W9-AAR-832

Middle Grades

**ASSESSMENT
PACKAGE**

1

BERKELEY

HARVARD

MICHIGAN STATE

SHELL CENTRE

**Balanced Assessment for the
Mathematics Curriculum**

Dale Seymour Publications®
Parsippany, New Jersey

Project Directors: Alan Schoenfeld
Hugh Burkhardt
Phil Daro
Jim Ridgway
Judah Schwartz
Sandra Wilcox

Managing Editors: Alan MacDonell and Catherine Anderson

Acquisitions Editor: Merle Silverman

Project Editor: Toni-Ann Guadagnoli

Production/Manufacturing Director: Janet Yearian

Senior Production/Manufacturing Coordinator: Fiona Santoianni

Design Director: Phyllis Aycock

Design Manager: Jeff Kelly

Cover and Interior Designer: Don Taka

Cover Image: Hutchings Photography

Illustrator: Larry Nolte

The work of this project was supported by a grant from the National Science Foundation.
The opinions expressed in these materials do not necessarily represent the position, policy,
or endorsement of the Foundation.

Dale Seymour Publications
An imprint of Pearson Learning
299 Jefferson Road, P.O. Box 480
Parsippany, New Jersey 07054-0480
www.pearsonlearning.com
1-800-321-3106

ISBN 0-7690-0066-5

4 5 6 7 8 9 10-ML-02-01

This Book Is Printed
On Recycled Paper

Authors

This assessment package was designed and developed by members of the Balanced Assessment Project team, particularly Judith Zawojewski, Mary Bouck, John Gillespie, Sandra Wilcox, Helene Alpert, Angela Krebs, Faaiz Gierdien, Whitney Johnson, and Kyle Ward. The editor was Mary Bouck.

Many others have made helpful comments and suggestions in the course of the development. We thank them all. The project is particularly grateful to the mathematics consultants, teachers, and students with whom these tasks were developed and tested, particularly Josh Coty, Ray Fauch, Julie Faulkner, Loraine Gawlik, Yvonne Grant, Lisa Harden, Liz Jones, Terri Keusch, Tom Little, Tammy McCarthy, Jan Palkowski, Marlene Robinson, Mark Rudd, Nancy Rudd, Mary Beth Schmitt, Janet Small, Judy Vandermeulen, Patti Wagner, and Mike Wilson.

The project was directed by Alan Schoenfeld, Hugh Burkhardt, Phil Daro, Jim Ridgway, Judah Schwartz, and Sandra Wilcox.

The package consists of materials compiled or adapted from work done at the four sites of the Balanced Assessment Project:

Balanced Assessment
Graduate School of Education
University of California
Berkeley, CA 94720-1670
USA

Balanced Assessment (MARS)
513 Erickson Hall
Michigan State University
East Lansing, MI 48824
USA

Balanced Assessment
Educational Technology Center
Harvard University
Cambridge, MA 02138
USA

Balanced Assessment
Shell Centre for Mathematical
Education
University of Nottingham
Nottingham NG7 2RD
England

Additional tasks and packages, the materials in their original form, and other assessment resources such as guides to scoring may be obtained from the project sites. For a full list of available publications, and for further information, contact the Project's Mathematics Assessment Resource Service (MARS) at the Michigan State address above. We welcome your comments.

Table of Contents

What is balanced assessment?

Mathematics assessments tell us and our students how well they are learning mathematics. A carefully designed mathematics assessment should:

- assess the mathematics that counts, focusing on important ideas and processes;

- be fair to the students, providing them with a set of opportunities to demonstrate what they know and can do;

- be fair to the curriculum, offering a balance of opportunities—long and short tasks, basic knowledge and problem solving, individual and group work, and the spectrum of concepts and processes that reflect the vision of the NCTM *Standards;*

- be of such high quality that students and teachers learn from them—so that assessment time serves as instructional time, and assessment and curriculum live in harmony;

- provide useful information to administrators, so they can judge the effectiveness of their programs; to teachers, so they can judge the quality of their instruction; and to students and parents, so they can see where the students are doing well and where more work is needed.

This is such an assessment package, dealing with the mathematics appropriate for the middle grades. It was designed by the Balanced Assessment Project, an NSF-supported collaboration that was funded to create a series of exemplary assessment items and packages for assessing students' mathematical performance at various grade levels (elementary grades, middle grades, high school, and advanced high school). Balanced Assessment offers a wide range of extensively field-tested tasks and packages—some paper-and-pencil, some high-tech or multimedia—and consulting services to help states and districts implement meaningful and informative mathematics assessments.

What is balance?

It's easy to see what isn't balanced. An assessment that focuses on computation only is out of balance. So is one that focuses on patterns, functions, and algebra to the exclusion of geometry, shape, and space, or that ignores or gives a cursory nod toward statistics and probability. Likewise, assessments that do not provide students with ample opportunity to show how they can reason or communicate mathematically are unbalanced. These are content and process dimensions of balance, but there are many others—length of task, whether tasks are pure or applied, and so on. The following table shows some of the dimensions used to design and balance this package. (For explanations of terms that may be unfamiliar, see the Glossary.)

Dimensions of Balance

Mathematical Content Dimension

- **Mathematical Content** will include some of the following:

  Number and Quantity including: concepts and representation; computation; estimation and measurement; number theory and general number properties.

  Patterns, Functions, and Algebra including: patterns and generalization; functional relationships (including ratio and proportion); graphical and tabular representation; symbolic representation; forming and solving relationships.

  Geometry, Shape, and Space including: shape, properties of shapes, relationships; spatial representation, visualization, and construction; location and movement; transformation and symmetry; trigonometry.

  Handling Data, Statistics, and Probability including: collecting, representing, and interpreting data; probability models—experimental and theoretical; simulation.

  Other Mathematics including: discrete mathematics, including combinatorics; underpinnings of calculus; mathematical structures.

Mathematical Process Dimension

- **Phases** of problem solving, reasoning, and communication will include, as broad categories, some or all of the following: modeling and formulating; transforming and manipulating; inferring and drawing conclusions; checking and evaluating; reporting.

Task Type Dimensions

- **Task Type** will be one of the following: open investigation; nonroutine problem; design; plan; evaluation and recommendation; review and critique; re-presentation of information; technical exercise; definition of concepts.

- **Nonroutineness** in: context; mathematical aspects or results; mathematical connections.

- **Openness:** It may have an open end with open questions; open middle.

- **Type of Goal** is one of the following: pure mathematics; illustrative application of the mathematics; applied power over the practical situation.

- **Reasoning Length** is the expected time for the longest section of the task. (It is an indication of the amount of "scaffolding"—the detailed step-by-step guidance that the prompt may provide.)

Circumstances of Performance Dimensions

- **Task Length:** ranging from short tasks (10–25 minutes), through long tasks (30–60 minutes), to extended tasks (several days to several weeks).

- **Modes of Presentation:** written; oral; video; computer.

- **Modes of Working** on the task: individual; group; mixed.

- **Modes of Response** by the student: written; built; spoken; programmed; performed.

What's in a package?

A typical Balanced Assessment Package offers ten to twenty tasks, ranging in length from 5 to 45 minutes. Some of the tasks consist of a single problem, while others consist of a sequence of problems. Taken together, the tasks provide students with an opportunity to display their knowledge and skills across the broad spectrum of content and processes described in the NCTM *Standards*. It takes time to get this kind of rich information—but the problems are mathematically rich and well worth the time spent on them.

What's included with each task?

We have tried to provide you with as much information as possible about the mathematics central to solving a task, about managing the assessment, and about typical student responses and how to analyze the mathematics in them. Each section of this package, corresponding to one task, consists of the following:

Overview   The first page of each section provides a quick overview that lets you see whether the task is appropriate for use at any particular point in the curriculum. This overview includes the following:

- Task Description—the situation that students will be asked to investigate or solve.

- Assumed Mathematical Background—the kinds of previous experiences students will need to have had to engage the task productively.

- Core Elements of Performance—the mathematical ideas and processes that will be central to the task.

- Circumstances—the estimated time for students to work on the task; the special materials that the task will require; whether students will work individually, in pairs, or in small groups; and any other such information.

Task Prompt   These pages are intended for the student. To make them easy to find, they have been designed with stars in the margin and a white bar across the top. The task prompt begins with a statement for the student characterizing the aims of the task. In some cases there is a pre-assessment activity that teachers assign in advance of the formal assessment. In some cases there is a launch activity that familiarizes students with the context but is not part of the formal assessment.

Sample Solution   Each task is accompanied by at least one solution; where there are multiple approaches to a problem, more than one may appear.

Using this Task   Here we provide suggestions about launching the task and helping students understand the context of the problem. Some tasks have pre-activities; some have students do some initial exploration in pairs or as a whole class to become familiar with the context while the formal assessment is done individually. Information from field-testing about challenging aspects of tasks is given here. We may also include suggestions for subsequent instruction related to the task, as well as extensions that can be used for assessment or instructional purposes.

Characterizing Performance   This section contains descriptions of characteristic student responses that the task is likely to elicit. These descriptions, based on the *Core Elements of Performance*, indicate various levels of successful engagement with the task. They are accompanied by annotated artists' renderings of typical student work. These illustrations will prepare you to assess the wide range of responses produced by your students. We have chosen examples that show something of the range and variety of responses to the task, and the various aspects of mathematical performance it calls for. The commentary is intended to exemplify these key aspects of performance at various levels across several domains. Teachers and others have found both the examples and the commentary extremely useful; its purpose is to bring out explicitly for each task the wide range of mathematical performance that the standards imply.

Scoring student work

The discussions of student work in the section *Characterizing Performance* are deliberately qualitative and holistic, avoiding too much detail. They are designed to focus on the mathematical ideas that "count," summarized in the *Core Elements of Performance* for each task. They offer a guide to help teachers and students look in some depth at a student's work in the course of instruction, considering how it might be improved.

For some other purposes, we need more. Formal assessment, particularly if the results are used for life-critical decisions, demands more accurate scoring, applied consistently across different scorers. This needs more precise rubrics, linked to a clear scheme for reporting on performance. These can be in a variety of styles, each of which has different strengths. The Balanced Assessment Project has developed resources that support a range of styles.

For example, *holistic approaches* require the scorer to take a balanced overall view of the student's response, relating general criteria of quality in performance to the specific item. *Point scoring approaches* draw attention in detail to the various aspects of performance that the task involves, provide a natural mechanism for balancing greater strength in one aspect with some weakness in another, and are useful for *aggregating scores*.

How to use this package

This assessment package may be used in a variety of ways, depending on your local needs and circumstances.

- You may want to implement formal performance assessment under controlled conditions at the school, district, or state level. This package provides a balanced set of tasks appropriate for such on-demand, high-stakes assessment.

- You may want to provide opportunities for classroom-based performance assessment, embedded within the curriculum, under less-controlled conditions. This package allows you the discretion of selecting tasks that are appropriate for use at particular points in the curriculum.

- You may be looking for tasks to serve as a transition toward a curriculum as envisioned in the NCTM *Standards* or as enrichment for existing curriculum. In this case, the tasks in this package can serve as rich instructional problems to enhance your curriculum. They are exemplars of the kinds of instructional tasks that will support performance assessment and can be used for preparing students for future performance assessment. Even in these situations, the tasks provide you with rich sites to engage in informal assessment of student understanding.

Preparing for the assessment

We urge you to work through a task yourself before giving it to your students. This gives you an opportunity to become familiar with the context and the mathematical demands of the task, and to anticipate what might need to be highlighted in launching the task.

It is important to have at hand all the necessary materials students need to engage a task before launching them on the task. We assume that students have certain tools and materials available at all times in the mathematics classroom and that these will be accessible to students to choose from during any assessment activity.

At the middle grades these resources include: grid paper and square and isometric dot paper; dice, square tiles, cubes, and other concrete materials; calculators; rulers, compasses, and protractors or angle rulers; scissors, markers, tape, string, paper clips, and glue.

If a task requires any special materials, these are specified in the task.

Managing the assessment

We anticipate that this package will be used in a variety of situations. Therefore, our guidance about managing assessment is couched in fairly general suggestions. We point out some considerations you may want to take into account under various circumstances.

The way in which any particular task is introduced to students will vary. The launch will be shaped by a number of considerations (for example, the students, the complexity of the instructions, the degree of familiarity students have with the context of the problem). In some cases it will be necessary only to distribute the task to students and then let them read and work through the task. Other situations may call for you to read the task to the class to assure that everyone understands the instructions, the context, and the aim of the assessment. Decisions of this kind will be influenced by the ages of the students, their experiences with reading mathematical tasks, their fluency in English, and any difficulties in reading that might exclude them from otherwise productively engaging with the mathematics of the task.

Under conditions of formal assessment, once students have been set to work on a task, you should not intervene except where specified. This is essential in formal, high-stakes assessment but it is important under any assessment circumstance. Even the slightest intervention—reinterpreting instructions, suggesting ways to begin, offering prompts when students appear to be stuck— has the potential to alter the task for the student significantly. However, you should provide general encouragement within a supportive classroom environment as a normal part of doing mathematics in school. This includes reminding students about the aim of the assessment (using the words at the beginning of the task prompt) when the period of assessment is nearing an end, and how to turn in their work when they have completed the task.

We suggest a far more relaxed use of the package when students are meeting these kinds of tasks for the first time, particularly in situations where they are being used primarily as learning tasks to enhance the curriculum. Under these circumstances you may reasonably decide to do some coaching, talk with students as they work on a task, pose questions when they seem to get stuck. In these instances you may be using the tasks for informal assessment—observing what strategies students favor, what kinds of questions they ask, what they seem to understand and what they are struggling with, what kinds of prompts get them unstuck. This can be extremely useful information in helping you make ongoing instructional and assessment decisions. However, as students have more experiences with these kinds of tasks, the amount of coaching you do should decline and students should rely less on this kind of assistance.

Under conditions of formal assessment, you will need to make decisions about how tasks will be scored and by whom, how scores will be aggregated across tasks, and how students' accomplishments will be reported to interested constituencies. These decisions will, of necessity, be made at the school, district, or state level and will likely reflect educational, political, and economic considerations specific to the local context.

Expanded Table of Contents *

Long Tasks	Task Type	Circumstances of Performance
1. Border Tiles	45-minute pure investigation; open-ended; nonroutine context, loosely related to adult life	individual assessment after a whole class introduction and some entry work in pairs
2. Table Tennis	45-minute nonroutine problem; applied power in a student-life context; nonroutine in both context and mathematical content	individual assessment after a whole class introduction
3. Consecutive Addends	60-minute pure investigation; open-ended nonroutine context	individual assessment after a whole class introduction
4. Emergency 911! Bay City	60-minute open-ended evaluation and recommendation problem; applied power in an adult-life, nonroutine context	pair assessment
5. Sum of Seven	30-minute evaluation problem; applied power in a student-life context, currently nonroutine	individual assessment
6. T-shirt Design	30-minute re-presentation of information; nonroutine open-ended problem; illustrative application	individual assessment after a whole class introduction
7. Energy	60-minute re-presentation of information; nonroutine open-ended problem; applied power in an adult-life context	individual assessment after a whole class introduction

* For explanations of terms that may be unfamiliar, see the Glossary, and the *Dimensions of Balance* table in the Introduction.

Mathematical Content	**Mathematical Processes**
Patterns and functions in a pure geometric context	formulation of relationships through conjecture, verification, and generalization; some manipulation
Other mathematics: a focus on combinatorics with some practical number work	formulation and manipulation are evenly balanced
Patterns and generalizations in a pure number context	formulation and modeling are used with some drawing of conclusions
Representing and interpreting data and statistics	inferring from given data and drawing conclusions with a written report
Finding and interpreting probabilities, either experimental or theoretical	modeling of a probability experiment
Locating and describing geometric shapes and space	modeling a way to describe a design and completing a written report
Data and statistics; designing a graph or visual representation of the data	interpretation of data and transformation from one representation to another

Expanded Table of Contents

Mathematical Content	Mathematical Processes
Handling data: a statistical analysis of 3 sets of 5 numbers, where spread is the dominant effect; associated number work	balances formulation, manipulation, and interpretation beyond the mechanical application of rules.
Number and quantity; working with rational numbers in a geometric context	manipulation of shapes and rational numbers, some checking and evaluation of work is required
Geometry, space, and shape; working with proportions and scaling in a geometric context; some generalization	mainly checking and evaluation
Number and quantity; adding decimals and producing solution sets that satisfy given constraints	formulation, manipulation, and checking of results
Geometry, space, and shape; using 3-D spatial reasoning and determining surface areas and volumes	representation of spatial information, modeling and formulation followed by manipulation
Algebra and functions; translation to numerical, graphical, and symbolic-algebra form of a verbal description of exponential behavior	mainly manipulation, with some formulation in the early parts

Mathematical Content	Mathematical Processes
Data and statistics link to the game's geometry in the design and evaluation of a game; simulation, collection of experimental data, and probability inferences for the shapes involved	a balance between formulation, manipulation, and interpretation, with evaluation of results

Border Tiles

Long Task

Task Description

This task asks students to investigate the use of different types of tiles to create rectangles with borders around their perimeter. Students form conjectures about patterns and rules for the number of tiles needed to make different classes of rectangles.

Assumed Mathematical Background

It is assumed that students have had experiences with open-ended problems that engage them in investigating a situation, making conjectures, searching for patterns, and drawing conclusions from their findings.

Core Elements of Performance

- identify classes of rectangles relevant to the investigation
- pose conjectures about rules that relate the number of tile-types needed to make different classes of rectangles
- systematically investigate the conjectures
- draw appropriate conclusions about the generalizability of the conjectures

Circumstances

Grouping:	Following a class introduction, students do some entry work in pairs, and then complete an individual written response.
Materials:	dot paper, graph paper, and models of tiles cut from transparency
Estimated time:	45 minutes

Border Tiles

As a class

When tiling walls and floors, sometimes people use special tiles that have borders on them. Square tiles can have borders on any number of edges. The six possible border tiles are shown below.

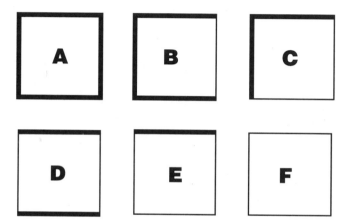

Each of these tiles can be flipped, or rotated, and still keep the same letter name. For example, the C-tile can look like any of the tiles shown here.

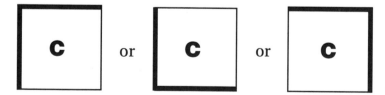

Some of these tiles can be placed together to make rectangles with dark borders around the perimeter. For example:

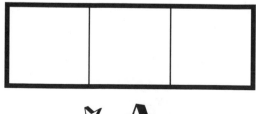

1. Luke calls the rectangle on the bottom of the previous page a 1-by-3 rectangle since it is one square tile wide and three square tiles long. How many of each type of tile are in this 1-by-3 rectangle? _____

2. How many of each type of tile would be in a 1-by-6 rectangle?_____

3. Luke noticed similarities in all of the rectangles that are one square tile wide. He created a class of rectangles he called "1-bys." For any rectangle in Luke's class of "1-bys," find how many of each type of tile would be needed. _____

_____

With a partner

Create a class of rectangles different from Luke's "1-bys." Look for a general rule that gives the number of each type of tile used in your class of rectangles.

This problem gives you the chance to

- *formulate conjectures*
- *systematically investigate conjectures*
- *find patterns and rules*
- *justify why the patterns and rules generalize across cases*

On your own

Write a general rule for the number of each type of tile in a class of rectangles.

Justify or explain why your rules work for all the rectangles in the class.

Do this for as many classes of rectangles as you can.

Name _____ Date _____

Border Tiles Transparency

Task

A Sample Solution

The following is an example of a drawing a student might do to investigate square rectangles.

```
A
```

```
C   C
C   C
```

```
C  E  C
E  F  E
C  E  C
```

```
C  E  E  C
E  F  F  E
E  F  F  E
C  E  E  C
```

```
C  E  E  E  C
E  F  F  F  E
E  F  F  F  E
E  F  F  F  E
C  E  E  E  C
```

```
C  E  E  E  E  C
E  F  F  F  F  E
E  F  F  F  F  E
E  F  F  F  F  E
C  E  E  E  E  C
```

The following table summarizes the results found by making squares.

	A	B	C	D	E	F
1-by-1	1	0	0	0	0	0
2-by-2	0	0	4	0	0	0
3-by-3	0	0	4	0	4	1
4-by-4	0	0	4	0	8	4
5-by-5	0	0	4	0	12	9
6-by-6	0	0	4	0	16	16
n-by-n (for $n \geq 2$)	0	0	4	0	$4(n-2)$	$(n-2)^2$

The following are some rules about the numbers of different types of tiles needed to make the class of rectangles that are squares.

A-tile: An A-tile makes a 1-by-1 square by itself. A-tiles are not used in any other squares.

B-tile: There are no B-tiles used in any squares since three of its sides are borders and adding another tile to complete the border would no longer make a square.

C-tile: These tiles are used to make the 4 corners of any rectangle that is not a "1-by," including squares that are at least 2-by-2.

D-tile: There are no D-tiles used in squares. D-tiles are only used in "1-bys."

E-tile: E-tiles are used as noncorner edge tiles of any rectangle that is not a "1-by," including squares. Starting with 4 E-tiles in a 3-by-3 square, the number of E-tiles increases to 8 tiles in a 4-by-4 square, 12 tiles in a 5-by-5 square, 16 tiles in a 6-by-6 square, and so on. As you increase the length of the square by one tile, 4 E-tiles are added to the figure—one to each side. For any n-by-n square with n greater than or equal to 2, there are $4(n-2)$ E-tiles.

F-tile: To make a 3-by-3 square, 1 F-tile is needed. Four F-tiles are needed in a 4-by-4 square, 9 F-tiles in a 5-by-5 square, 16 F-tiles in a 6-by-6 square, and so on. Since F-tiles are the "inside" pieces, they form a square inside the original square. For any n-by-n square with n greater than or equal to 2, there are $(n-2)^2$ F-tiles.

Task

The following are some results found when investigating the class of 2-by-n rectangles.

A-tile: No 2-by-n rectangle can contain an A-tile; an A-tile makes a square by itself because all of its edges are borders.

B-tile: The 2-by-n B-tiles can only be used in a 2-by-1 rectangle. This rectangle uses exactly two B-tiles.

C-tile: Since the C-tile is a corner tile, all 2-by-n rectangles, where n is greater than 1, contain exactly 4 C-tiles.

D-tile: Since D-tiles can only be used in the class of 1-by-n rectangles of $n > 2$ (because the opposite edges are borders), there will be no D-tiles in 2-by-n rectangles.

E-tile: The number of E-tiles in a 2-by-n rectangle, where n is greater than 1, will always be $2(n-2)$. Each row has n tiles, 2 of these tiles are C-tiles, and the others are E-tiles because only one edge is a border. Since there are two rows of C-tiles and E-tiles, the total number of E-tiles will be $2(n-2)$.

F-tile: The 2-by-n class of rectangles will not have any F-tiles. Because F-tiles do not have a border, they are used "inside" rectangles and thus are only used in m-by-n rectangles where m and n are both greater than or equal to 3.

Students' investigations can include multiple dimensions of rectangles. For a correct solution, students need to identify a class of rectangles to consider (for example, squares, 2-bys), and then investigate how many of the different types of tiles are used in the class. Based on their investigations, students must describe the patterns they find and pose rules. Students' work should show evidence of conducting systematic investigations such as testing a variety of cases for a given class of rectangles, searching for a counterexample, and making deductive arguments. Finally, students should draw appropriate conclusions about their rules based on the investigations they have conducted. For example, if students find one counterexample, they may conclude that the rule does not hold. They may even go on to identify under what conditions the rule holds and under what conditions it does not hold.

More on the Mathematics

The following solution summarizes the rules for all n by m rectangles:

$n = m = 1$	1 A-tile
$n = 1, m > 1$	2 B-tiles, $(m - 2)$ D-tiles
$n > 1, m > 1$	4 C-tiles, $[2(n + m) - 8]$ E-tiles, $[(n - 2)(m - 2)]$ F-tiles

Using this Task

Before administering this assessment you may want to make and cut out the border tiles from the sheet included (see page 5). Dot and graph paper are included in the activity and should be available for students to use.

To launch the task, distribute the first two pages of the task to students. Read aloud the top of the first page and address the first question on the second page as a class. Have students label each piece in the given rectangle to help them understand that orientation does not make a tile different (this drawing contains only B-tiles and a D-tile). Students should work in pairs on questions 2 and 3 for no more than 3-4 minutes. Have some of the students share their responses to these questions with the class to make certain that all students understand how the tiles are used.

Continue the launch by reading with the class the instructions for *With a partner* and then give students no more than 15 minutes to work in pairs to brainstorm patterns or rules to investigate. Make sure students understand what is meant by a "class of rectangles." You may want to reiterate that Luke found a class of rectangles that he called "1-bys."

After students have explored the problem with a partner, distribute the individual assessment sheet entitled *On your own*. Read aloud the aims of the assessment found in the box on the top of page 4. Students should then work individually for at least 20 minutes. The individual work will be assessed.

Issues for Classroom Use

Posing and investigating conjectures and searching for ways to verify whether and under what conditions a conjecture holds is part of the essence of mathematics. Students who have had little experience with open-ended investigations may have difficulty starting this task and sustaining effort.

Students may have difficulty determining whether or not a pattern or rule can be generalized to all cases. Frequently, students test strategically selected cases and then claim with certainty that the pattern or rule holds true for *all* cases. In fact, given the extent of their investigations students can claim that the conjecture seems to be valid, but may not necessarily be true for all cases. A generalization for cases can be made either by testing every case (in a finite set of cases), by making a deductive argument (using natural and/or symbolic language), or by finding a counterexample (in which case the rule or pattern does not hold).

Characterizing Performance

This section offers a characterization of student responses and provides indications of the ways in which the students were successful or unsuccessful in engaging with and completing the task. The descriptions are keyed to the *Core Elements of Performance.* Our global descriptions of student work range from "The student needs significant instruction" to "The student's work meets the essential demands of the task." Samples of student work that exemplify these descriptions of performance are included below, accompanied by commentary on central aspects of each student's response. These sample responses are *representative;* they may not mirror the global description of performance in all respects, being weaker in some and stronger in others.

The characterization of student responses for this task is based on these *Core Elements of Performance:*

1. Identify classes of rectangles relevant to the investigation.
2. Pose conjectures about rules that relate the number of tile-types needed to make different classes of rectangles.
3. Systematically investigate the conjectures.
4. Draw appropriate conclusions about the generalizability of the conjectures.

Descriptions of Student Work

The student needs significant instruction.

Student shows evidence of a search but states no rule(s), states incorrect/incomplete rule(s), or states only rule(s) for "1-bys."

Student A

Student A shows evidence of searching for a pattern, but only for the "1-by-n" rectangles that were investigated in the pre-assessment activity. The rule posed by Student A is incomplete "2 B's + # D's = # tiles." Although implicit in the rule is that every "1-by-x" rectangle has 2 B-tiles in it, the rule doesn't provide a way to generate the number of D-tiles given information about the dimensions of a "1-by" rectangle.

The student needs some instruction.

Task
1

Student poses at least two plausible rules for cases beyond the "1-bys." There is an attempt to justify the rules, but the support is nonexistent or weak (for example, the student does not test an adequate number or variety of cases for the conclusion drawn; student does not delineate the rectangles for which the rules hold).

Student B

Student B considers all six tiles. However, only the rules for tiles B and C implicitly address the number of tiles used for a class of rectangles, as requested in the directions. The rules for D-, E-, and F-tiles address when the tiles are used and when they are not. The class of rectangles for the A-tiles and C-tiles refer to classes different from the "1-bys," but the student provides weak support for each of the rules: only one example of each is considered on the dot paper. Student B correctly rules out appropriate cases for tiles A, C, D, E, and F, but for tile B, the student neglects to mention that the rule does not hold for 1-by-1 rectangles. To have made a score at the next higher level, the student would need to provide strong support for at least two of the rules.

The student's work needs to be revised.

Student poses at least two complete and correct rules about the number of tiles needed for classes of rectangles, and at least one rule is for a class beyond the "1-bys." (There may also be some incomplete or incorrect rules.) The student also provides *strong* support for the plausibility of at least two of the rules: he or she tests an adequate number and variety of cases and delineates the cases for which the rules hold. (There may be some errors and omissions.)

Student C

Student C makes rules about five tiles: B, D, C, E, and F. The rules for tile B and tile D are clear and correct for the "1-by" class of rectangles, and *generalized* reasoning is used to support the rule for the B- and D-tiles. The rule for C-tiles is clear and correct for both the "2-by" and "3-by" rectangles, and strong support for the C-tiles rule is made in the table for the "3-by" class of rectangles. Although the rules for tiles E and F do not make it possible to generate the number of tiles given the dimensions of the rectangle, the patterns of increase are correctly related to incremental increases in one dimension of the "3-by" rectangle. Although the rules for the E-tile and F-tile are incomplete, they are plausible rules, and the student provides support for the plausibility of the E and F rules in the table of "3-by" test cases. Finally, Student C clearly describes the cases for which the B-, D-, and C-tiles' rules hold, by ruling out the appropriate cases.

Task 1

The student's work meets the essential demands of the task.

Student poses at least two complete and correct rules about the number of tiles needed for a class of rectangles beyond the "1-bys." The student also provides *generalizable* support for at least two of the rules: explains why the rules hold for all rectangles in the class, and delineates the cases for which the rules hold.

Student D

Student D investigates the class of square and poses correct and complete rules for tiles C, E, and F. The explanations given are *generalizable* to all members of the class.

Student A

#3

#B	1 By X
2	1 By 2
2	1 By 3
2	1 By 4
2	1 By 5
2	1 By 6
2	1 By 7

#D	1 By X
0	2
1	3
2	4
3	5
4	6
5	7

So 2 B's + #D's = # tiles
tiles is = to x in 1 By X
Since It's One times the tiles
in length

A tiles: these tiles are only used in a 1 by 1 rectangle

B tiles: these are only used in 1 by — rectangles and are on opposite ends of the rectangles

C tiles: these tiles are used as corners and only occur in a 2 by 2 or larger rectangle.

D tiles: these tiles are used in a 1 by situation but are never found in 1 by 1 rectangles.

E tiles: these tiles are used in rectangles equal to or larger than 2 by 3 rectangles.

F tiles: these tiles have no border and are sanwiched between other tiles it only occurs in rectangles 3 by 3 or larger.

See Grid for Examples

Student B

A

B   B

C   C

C   C

D

E E
E   E
E   E
E E

F F F
F F F
F F F

Rule for 1-by,

For every "1-by", except for 1x1, there are 2 b tiles. All the tiles in between the 2 b's are d's. When you add the b's to the d's you should get the # of tiles in the rectangle.

Rule for 2-by

For every "2-by", except for 2x1, there are 4 c's. As each 2-by increases, the e tiles increase by 2, starting at zero.

Rule for 3-by

The rule for 3-by's is exactly the same as the rule for the 2-by's but starting with 2. In 3-by's.

Rule for 4-by

Same as 3-by rule.

3 by 5	a	b	c	d	e	f
3 X 1		Z		1		
3 X 2			4	4	Z	
3 X 3			4		4	1
3 X 4			4		6	2
3 X 5			4		8	3
3 X 6			4		10	4
3 X 7			4		12	5
3 X 8			4		14	6
3 X 9			4		16	7
3 X 10			4		18	8
3 X 11			4		20	9
3 X 12			4		22	10

For every "3-by", except for 3x1, there are 4 c's. As each 3-by increases, the e tiles increase by Z. From 3x3 on there are f tiles too that increase by 1 for every increase of the 3-by's.

Student D

Squares:

Table A: Squares			
Sides	C	E	F	TOTAL
2X2	4	0	0	4
3X3	4	4	1	9
4X4	4	8	4	16
5X5	4	12	9	25
6X6	4	16	16	36
7X7	4	20	25	49
8X8	4	24	36	64
9X9	4	28	49	81
10X10	4	32	64	100

Connections: A is only used in the first square so I didn't put it in the table. C always remains as 4 because no matter how the Perimeter changes, a square always has 5 4 corners. E changes by 4 every trial because if one side changes by one, then the total change is 4 (4 sides to a square). F is the length of one side (minus the corners) times the length of the other side (they're all equal any ways!) –minus the corners.

EXAMPLES →

So if you take 2 away From the numbers of tiles on a side E is 4 times that.

2

Design and apply a method for counting.

Table Tennis

Long Task

Task Description

This task asks students to determine how many matches and how much time are needed to run a round-robin table tennis tournament, in which each player is matched in turn against every other player.

Assumed Mathematical Background

It is assumed that students have had experience conducting systematic investigations.

Core Elements of Performance

- design a method for determining the number of games in a round-robin tournament
- analyze and convert among units of measure to determine the amount of time needed for a tournament

Circumstances

Grouping:	Following a class introduction, students complete an individual written response.
Materials:	No special materials are needed for this task.
Estimated time:	45 minutes

Table Tennis

As a class

You have the job of organizing a round-robin table tennis competition for some students in your class. All the matches are singles—one against one.

A round-robin competition means that every player has to play every other player once.

You find out that there are four tables available, in the large hall at the local sports club. Individual table tennis matches normally take about half an hour.

Imagine there are just three people in the competition. Each person has to play every other person once.
How many matches will be played in the tournament? _____

Name	Date

This problem gives you the chance to

- *design a method for finding the number of games*
- *reason with units of measure*

On your own

1. Ten people want to sign up to be in the competition.

   a. How many matches will be played altogether? _____

   b. Explain how you worked out your answer.

2. Individual table tennis matches usually take half an hour. Remember there are four tables available. Determine the shortest amount of time for the competition. (Show all of your work.)

3. Suppose two additional students decide to join the tournament.

   a. How long will the tournament now take? _____

   b. Explain how you worked out your answer.

Task 2 A Sample Solution

1a. 45 matches.

1b. Here are three possible methods for determining how many matches will be played.

   i. An organized list could be used.
We could label the players A, B, C, D, E, F, G, H, I, and J.
AB, AC, AD, AE, AF, AG, AH, AI, AJ
BC, BD, BE, BF, BG, BH, BI, BJ
CD, CE, CF, CG, CH, CI, CJ
DE, DF, DG, DH, DI, DJ
EF, EG, EH, EI, EJ
FG, FH, FI, FJ
GH, GI, GJ
HI, HJ
IJ

   ii. A second method is to make a chart using an "X" to keep track of the matches.

	A	B	C	D	E	F	G	H	I	J
A		X	X	X	X	X	X	X	X	X
B			X	X	X	X	X	X	X	X
C				X	X	X	X	X	X	X
D					X	X	X	X	X	X
E						X	X	X	X	X
F							X	X	X	X
G								X	X	X
H									X	X
I										X
J										

iii. The third method is to "reason through."
Player A plays 9 others; B has already played A but has 8 others to play; C has played A and B, but has 7 others to play, and so on. The total number of games = 9 + 8 + 7 + 6 + 5 + 4 + 3 + 2 + 1 = 45.

Task

2. If 4 matches can be played simultaneously in one half hour, then 8 matches can be played in 1 hour. Since there are 45 matches: 45 matches ÷ 8 matches/hour = 5 hours with a remainder of 5 matches. If 40 matches take 5 hours and the remaining 5 matches take 1 additional hour, then the total tournament time is 6 hours.

OR

45 matches ÷ (4 matches/half hour) = 11 half hours with a remainder of 1 match. If 44 matches take $5\frac{1}{2}$ hours and the remaining match takes one half hour, then the total time for the tournament is 6 hours.

3a. For 12 players (using any of the methods for solutions to question 1) there are 66 total matches.

3b. 66 matches ÷ 8 matches/hour = 8 hours with a remainder of 2 matches. If 64 matches take 8 hours and the remaining 2 matches take an additional half hour, then the total time for the tournament is $8\frac{1}{2}$ hours.

OR

66 matches ÷ 4 matches/half hour = 16 half hours with a remainder of 2 matches. If 64 matches take 8 hours and the remaining 2 matches take one half hour, then the total time for the tournament is $8\frac{1}{2}$ hours.

Task

Using this Task

Read and discuss the first page of the activity with the class. You may need to explain the idea of a round-robin competition, in which everyone plays everyone else. One way to increase the students' understanding of the situation is to have them role play and act out a three-person tournament, keeping track of which players play each other and how many total matches are played.

When it is clear to you that students understand the context, begin the individual assessment by reviewing with students the aims of the assessment given in the box at the top of the page entitled, *On your own*. Remind the students that only four tables can be used at any one time.

You may wish to extend this task by asking students to try to match up players to see which 4 pairs will play simultaneously during each half hour. This is a tricky problem because although each player plays every other player once, he or she can only play one game per half hour. Below is a list of possible match-ups for each set of 4 matches (numbered 1–12). You may want to challenge your students by asking them to create such a list.

	Table 1	Table 2	Table 3	Table 4
Match 1	B & I	C & H	D & G	E & F
Match 2	A & I	B & H	C & J	D & F
Match 3	A & H	B & J	C & I	D & E
Match 4	A & G	B & F	C & E	D & J
Match 5	A & F	B & G	D & I	E & J
Match 6	A & E	C & G	D & H	F & J
Match 7	A & D	C & F	E & I	G & J
Match 8	A & C	B & E	F & I	H & J
Match 9	A & B	C & D	E & H	G & I
Match 10	A & J	B & D	F & G	H & I
Match 11	B & C	E & G	F & H	I & J
Match 12	G & H			

Characterizing Performance

This section offers a characterization of student responses and provides indications of the ways in which the students were successful or unsuccessful in engaging with and completing the task. The descriptions are keyed to the *Core Elements of Performance.* Our global descriptions of student work range from "The student needs significant instruction" to "The student's work meets the essential demands of the task." Samples of student work that exemplify these descriptions of performance are included below, accompanied by commentary on central aspects of each student's response. These sample responses are *representative;* they may not mirror the global description of performance in all respects, being weaker in some and stronger in others.

The characterization of student responses for this task is based on these *Core Elements of Performance:*

1. Design a method for determining the number of games in a round-robin tournament.
2. Analyze and convert among units of measure to determine the amount of time needed for a tournament.

Descriptions of Student Work

The student needs significant instruction.

Student engages in the problem but does not use a reasonable method to determine both the number of games and the time needed.

Student A

Student A shows no evidence of methods used to determine either the number of games or the time needed.

The student needs some instruction.

Student uses a correct method to determine either the number of games *or* the time needed, but may make some errors in carrying them out (possibly resulting in a wrong answer).

Student B

Student B uses a diagram to find the number of games for 10 people and extends the method by using an organized list to find the number of additional games needed for adding 2 new players. However, Student B does not show evidence of a correct method for determining the amount of time needed for the tournament.

Student C

Student C describes a correct method for counting the games. To determine the time needed for the tournament, Student C does some correct arithmetic; however, this method does not attend to the half-hour unit of time per game. This problem persists in her response to question 3.

The student's work needs to be revised.

Student uses a correct method to determine both the number of games *and* the time needed and may make some errors in carrying them out (possibly resulting in a wrong answer).

Student D

Student D correctly uses a listing method to determine the number of games. He also uses a correct method for finding the time needed for a 10-person competition. One can assume he used some mental arithmetic to determine that an additional half hour was needed, for a total of 6 hours. However, in finding the number and time needed for a 12-member league, he gives the correct number of matches (but shows no evidence of how he arrived at that answer) and gives an incorrect answer for the time needed to run the competition. The reasoning presented neither matches a correct solution for the time of the competition nor either of the answers he has given. (He leaves out 6 matches in his diagram.) Student D may have performed some mental computations, adding an additional half hour to determine the time needed for the 12-person competition. Had Student D's reasoning been made explicit, then the work might have been considered as *meeting the essential demands of the task.*

Student E

Student E uses a reasonable method to determine the number of games in question 1. She also performs correct computations in determining the number of time needed to play the tournaments in questions 2 and 3. However, in this situation, it is not reasonable to play for "8:15 min"; total time must be in half-hour increments.

The student's work meets the essential demands of the task.

Student uses a correct method to determine both the number of games *and* the time needed with no errors in carrying them out. Some computational inaccuracies are okay.

Student F

Student F uses correct methods for determining both number of games and time needed to play the two tournaments and computes these answers correctly. For example, she determines that in 11 rounds or 11 half hours, 44 matches will be played. One additional match will require an additional half hour.

Student A

> **The problem gives you the chance to**
>
> ■ *design a method for finding the number of games*
> ■ *reason with units of measure*

On your own

1. Ten people want to sign up to be in the competition.
   a. How many matches will be played altogether? 42
   b. Explain how you worked out your answer. I put down All ten NAMes and made A chart.

2. Individual table tennis matches usually take half an hour. Remember there are four tables available. Determine the shortest amount of time for the competition. (Show all of your work.)

   12 hours and 60 minutes 42+30 because there Are 42 mAtches and eAch tAkes 30 minutes,

3. Suppose two additional students decide to join the tournament.
   a. How long will the tournament now take?
   b. Explain how you worked out your answer. 15 hours because there Are 50 mAtches times a hAlf an hour each at 30

1. Ten people want to sign up to be in the competition.
   a. How many matches will be played altogether? 45
   b. Explain how you worked out your answer.

   drew 10 lines, drew a line to each person that they had to play

   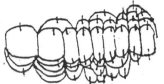

2. Individual table tennis matches usually take half an hour.
   Remember there are four tables available. Determine the shortest
   amount of time for the competition. (Show all of your work.)

   11 matches
   one match left

   $(11 \times .5) + 2.5$

   Divide all
   into 4

3. Suppose two additional students decide to join the tournament.
   a. How long will the tournament now take?
   b. Explain how you worked out your answer.

   1-11   8-11   5-12
   2-11   9-11   6-12
   3-11   10-11 7-12
   4-11   1-12   8-12
   5-11   2-12   9-12
   6-11   3-12   10-12
   7-11   4-12   11-12

   66

The problem gives you the chance to

- *design a method for finding the number of games*
- *reason with units of measure*

On your own

1. Ten people want to sign up to be in the competition.

   a. How many matches will be played altogether? **45**

   b. Explain how you worked out your answer.

   A 9 F 4
   B 8 G 3 } Mentally ✳ For Explanation
   C 7 H 2 } Thought   see Notebook paper
   D 6 I 1 } of.
   E 5 J 0

   $9+8+7+6+5+4+3+2+1+0 = 45$ matches

2. Individual table tennis matches usually take half an hour.
   Remember there are four tables available. Determine the shortest
   amount of time for the competition. (Show all of your work.)

   45 matches
   4 tables/1 match per
   4 matches/½ hr.

   $45 \div 4 = 11.25$ hours
   But you can't finish a match
   in 15 minutes, so round to 11.5 hours

   11.5 hours

3. Suppose two additional students decide to join the tournament.

   a. How long will the tournament now take?

   b. Explain how you worked out your answer.

   $11+10+9+8+7+6+5+4+3+2+1+0 = 66$ matches
   $66 \div 4 = 16.5$ hours for 66 matches.
   $16.5 - 11.5 =$ 5 hours more to add 2 more players

Student C

(2) b) Explanation — playing who?

who	A	B	C	D	E	F	G	H	I	J
A		X	X	X	X	X	X	X	X	X
B			X	X	X	X	X	X	X	X
C				X	X	X	X	X	X	X
D					X	X	X	X	X	X
E						X	X	X	X	X
F							X	X	X	X
G								X	X	X
H									X	X
I										X
J										

(3) b) Explanation — playing who?

who	A	B	C	D	E	F	G	H	I	J	K	L
A		X	X	X	X	X	X	X	X	X	X	X
B			X	X	X	X	X	X	X	X	X	X
C				X	X	X	X	X	X	X	X	X
D					X	X	X	X	X	X	X	X
E						X	X	X	X	X	X	X
F							X	X	X	X	X	X
G								X	X	X	X	X
H									X	X	X	X
I										X	X	X
J											X	X
K												X
L												

> **The problem gives you the chance to**
>
> ■ *design a method for finding the*
>   *number of games*
>
> ■ *reason with units of measure*

On your own

1. Ten people want to sign up to be in the competition.

   a. How many matches will be played altogether?

   b. Explain how you worked out your answer. 45

Skip
Numbers
So they
repeat the
play.

1.2 1.3 1.4 1.5 1.6 1.7 1.8 1.9 1.10   7.8 7.9
2.3 2.4 25 2.6 2.7 2.8 2.9 2.10   7.10
3.4 3.5 3.6 3.7 3.8 3.9 3.10   8.9 8.10
4.5 4.6 4.7 4.8 4.9 4.10   6.7 6.8
   5.6 5.7 5.8 5.9 5.10   6.9 6.10
                                                9

2. Individual table tennis matches usually take half an hour.

   Remember there are four tables available. Determine the shortest

   amount of time for the competition. (Show all of your work.)

4-30
4-30
4-30 minutes   4-30   6 hours
4-30   4.30
4-30   4.30
4-30   4-30
4-30   4.30

3. Suppose two additional students decide to join the tournament.

   a. How long will the tournament now take?

   b. Explain how you worked out your answer.

4.30   4-30
4-30   4-30
4-30
4-30   4-30
4-30
4-30   4-30   66 matches
4-30   4-30
4-30   8 hours
4-30
4-30

Student E

The problem gives you the chance to

- *design a method for finding the number of games*
- *reason with units of measure*

On your own

1. Ten people want to sign up to be in the competition.

    a. How many matches will be played altogether?

    b. Explain how you worked out your answer.   45

    I made a graph to show my work. In this graph, everyone played everyone else, but if 10 for instance dropped out of the tournament, then 9 would have to pick up playing when 10 lost or left off.

2. Individual table tennis matches usually take half an hour.

    Remember there are four tables available. Determine the shortest amount of time for the competition. (Show all of your work.) 6 hours

    45 games x30 mins = 1,350.   1,350 ÷ 60 (1 hour) = 22:30min

    22:30 ÷ 4 (tables) = about 6 hours.

3. Suppose two additional students decide to join the tournament.

    a. How long will the tournament now take? 8:15 min.

    b. Explain how you worked out your answer.

    66 games ÷ :30 min = 3.3 hours ÷ 4 = 8:15 hours at the most.

    I made a graph counted everything on the graph up, and came up with the fact that it would take at the most 8:15 min. to compete the entire tournament.

Student E

#1

10,9	9,8	8,7	7,6	6,5	5,4	4,3	3,2	2,1
10,8	9,7	8,6	7,5	6,4	5,3	4,2	3,1	
10,7	9,6	8,5	7,4	6,3	5,2	4,1		
10,6	9,5	8,4	7,3	6,2	5,1			
10,5	9,4	8,3	7,2	6,1				
10,4	9,3	8,2	7,1					
10,3	9,2	8,1						
10,2	9,1							
10,1								

#3

12,11	11,10	10,9	9,8	8,7	7,6	6,5	5,4	4,3	3,2	2,1
12,10	11,9	10,8	9,7	8,6	7,5	6,4	5,3	4,2	3,1	
12,9	11,8	10,7	9,6	8,5	7,4	6,3	5,2	4,1		
12,8	11,7	10,6	9,5	8,4	7,3	6,2	5,1			
12,7	11,6	10,5	9,4	8,3	7,2	6,1				
12,6	11,5	10,4	9,3	8,2	7,1					
12,5	11,4	10,3	9,2	8,1						
12,4	11,3	10,2	9,1							
12,3	11,2	10,1								
12,2	11,1									
12,1										

Student F

> **The problem gives you the chance to**
>
> ▪ *design a method for finding the number of games*
> ▪ *reason with units of measure*

On your own $9+8+7+6+5+4+3+2+1=45$

1. Ten people want to sign up to be in the competition.

   a. How many matches will be played altogether? 45

   b. Explain how you worked out your answer.

9=A	AB	BC	CD	DE	EF	FG	GH	
8=B	AC	BD	CE	DF	EG	FH	GI	
7=C	AD	BE	CF	DG	EH	FI	GJ③	
6=D	AE	BF	CG	DH	EI	FJ④		
5=E	AF	BG	CH	DI	EJ⑤			
4=F	AG	BH	CI	DJ⑥				
3=G	AH	BI	CJ⑦		HI			
2=H	AI⑨	BJ⑧			HJ②			
1=I	AJ⑩							
10=J								

If Ⓐ play = Ⓕ then it would be the same as Ⓕ playing Ⓐ

$y = \frac{1}{2}x^2 + \frac{1}{2}x$ Equation

Don't repeat combos !! ☺

2. Individual table tennis matches usually take half an hour. Remember there are four tables available. Determine the shortest amount of time for the competition. (Show all of your work.)

$45 \div 4 = 11.25$ $4 \times 11 = 44$ Ⓡ①

12 half hours (6 hrs.)

$11+10+9+8+7+6+5+4+3+2+1 = 66$

3. Suppose two additional students decide to join the tournament.

   a. How long will the tournament now take?

   b. Explain how you worked out your answer.

$66 \div 4 = 16.5$ $16 \times 4 = 64$ R2

$17 \div 2 = $ (8½ hrs.)

66 even tho' you have two left over you will have 4 open tables so... only an extra half hour still !

3

Consecutive Addends

Overview

Search for patterns of consecutive addends. Describe and explain patterns.

Long Task

Task Description

Students investigate numbers that can be expressed as sums of consecutive addends. They search for patterns, make generalizations about the patterns they find, and explain why they think the patterns occur.

Assumed Mathematical Background

It is assumed that students are familiar with number properties and have had experiences with conducting systematic investigations.

Core Elements of Performance

- systematically investigate consecutive addends
- find patterns about which numbers can be expressed as sums of different numbers of consecutive addends
- formulate generalizations about the patterns, using symbolic or natural language
- hypothesize about why these patterns occur

Circumstances

Grouping:	Following a class introduction, students complete an individual written response.
Materials:	two to three additional sheets of paper per student
Estimated time:	60 minutes

Consecutive Addends

As a class

The number 15 can be written as a sum of consecutive whole numbers in three different ways:

$$15 = 7 + 8$$
$$15 = 1 + 2 + 3 + 4 + 5$$
$$15 = 4 + 5 + 6$$

The number 9 can be written as a sum of consecutive whole numbers in two ways:

$$9 = 2 + 3 + 4$$
$$9 = 4 + 5$$

What are some other numbers that can be written as a sum of consecutive whole numbers?

This problem gives you the chance to

- *systematically look for patterns*
- *describe patterns*
- *generalize about patterns*
- *explain why patterns work*

On your own
(on a separate sheet of paper)

1. Look at other numbers and find out all you can about writing them as sums of consecutive whole numbers. You may want to start with the numbers from 1 to 36.

2. Decide what kinds of numbers can be written as a sum of 2 consecutive whole numbers; of 3 consecutive whole numbers; of 4 consecutive whole numbers; and so on.

3. What numbers cannot be written as a sum of consecutive whole numbers?

4. **a.** What patterns did you notice in exploring questions 1 through 3?
   b. Why do you think the patterns occur?

Task **A Sample Solution**

3

The following demonstrates a good basic solution that middle-grade students may give. However, depending on their prior mathematical experiences, students may bring additional mathematical ideas to bear on the task. For further information about the mathematical possibilities this task offers, please see the section *More on the Mathematics* following the sample solution.

1. Students may approach their investigations in different ways. One systematic way involves looking at the numbers in order starting from 1 and searching for all the possible ways to write each number as the sum of consecutive addends. Another way is to look at all the sums of two consecutive addends, then at the sums of three consecutive addends, then four, and so on. Still another way is to look at all the strings of consecutive addends that begin with 1, then all the strings of consecutive addends that begin with 2, and so on. The following chart shows all the possible ways to write the numbers 1 to 36 as the sum of consecutive positive whole number addends.

Number of consecutive addends

Sum	2	3	4	5	6	7	8
1							
2							
3	1+2						
4							
5	2+3						
6		1+2+3					
7	3+4						
8							
9	4+5	2+3+4					
10			1+2+3+4				
11	5+6						
12		3+4+5					
13	6+7						
14			2+3+4+5				
15	7+8	4+5+6		1+2+3+4+5			
16							
17	8+9						
18		5+6+7	3+4+5+6				
19	9+10						
20				2+3+4+5+6			

Number of consecutive addends

Sum	2	3	4	5	6	7	8
21	10+11	6+7+8			1+2+3+4+5+6		
22		4+5+6+7					
23	11+12						
24		7+8+9					
25	12+13			3+4+5+6+7			
26			5+6+7+8				
27	13+14	8+9+10			2+3+4+5+6+7		
28						1+2+3+4+5+6+7	
29	14+15						
30		9+10+11	6+7+8+9	4+5+6+7+8			
31	15+16						
32							
33	16+17	10+11+12			3+4+5+6+7+8		
34			7+8+9+10				
35	17+18			5+6+7+8+9		2+3+4+5+6+7+8	
36		11+12+13					1+2+3+4+5+6+7+8

Students sometimes consider 0 a possible addend, allowing 1 to be written as the sum of two addends, $1 = 0 + 1$. But they often do not include 0 consistently (for example, they may not say that $3 = 0 + 1 + 2$). It is appropriate and reasonable to include 0 consistently and possible in doing so to maintain generalizable patterns for the sums of different numbers of consecutive addends.

2. Numbers that can be written as the sum of **two** consecutive addends are all the odd numbers starting with 3: 3, 5, 7, 9, 11, 13, and so on. (includes 1 if 0 is considered as an addend). This pattern can be generalized as **3 + 2n**, where **n** is a nonnegative integer.

Numbers that can be written as the sum of **three** consecutive addends are the multiples of 3, beginning with 6: 6, 9, 12, 15, 18, 21, 24, and so on. (includes 3 if 0 is considered as an addend). This pattern can be generalized as **3x** where **x** is an integer greater than or equal to 2. It could also be written as **6 + 3n**, where **n** is a nonnegative integer.

Numbers that can be written as the sum of **four** consecutive addends include: 10, 14, 18, 22, 26, 30, 34, and so on (includes 6 if 0 is considered as an addend). This pattern can be generalized as **10 + 4n**, where **n** is a nonnegative integer.

Numbers that can be written as the sum of **five** consecutive addends include all the multiples of 5 starting with 15: 15, 20, 25, 30, 35, and so on (includes 10 if 0 is considered as an addend). This pattern can be generalized as **15 + 5n**, where **n** is a nonnegative integer.

Task

3

3. Numbers that cannot be written as the sum of consecutive addends are all the powers of 2: 1, 2, 4, 8, 16, 32, etc. (1 is not included if 0 is considered as an addend). This pattern can be generalized as 2^n where n is a nonnegative integer.

4. This question asks for patterns; a response here could include generalizations like those given above. The question also asks why these patterns occur.

When we add two consecutive whole numbers, we in effect add the same number twice plus 1. Two times any number yields an even number. Adding 1 makes the sum odd. This explains why all the sums of two consecutive addends are odd. It also explains why any odd number can be written as the sum of two consecutive addends. Simply subtract 1 and divide by 2 and the addends will be revealed. For example, to find two consecutive addends that will yield 87, subtract 1 (86) and then divide by 2 (43). Thus 87 can be expressed as 43 + 44.

Furthermore, as we add consecutive pairs of addends, we notice that our sums increase by 2 (see examples to the right). This occurs because, in effect, we add 1 to each addend or 2 altogether. We can observe these same patterns with any other numbers of consecutive addends.

$3 = 1 + 2$
      $+1 \ +1$
$5 = 2 + 3$
      $+1 \ +1$
$7 = 3 + 4$
      $+1 \ +1$
$9 = 4 + 5$

When we add three consecutive addends, we are actually adding the middle number three times; we can subtract 1 from the last addend and add it to the first. For example, 9 + 10 + 11 becomes 10 + 10 + 10. This also explains why any multiple of 3, starting with 6, can be written as the sum of three consecutive addends. Divide by 3, add 1, and subtract 1 and you have your addends. For example, since 414 ÷ 3 = 138, the three consecutive addends that will give you 414 are 137, 138, and 139.

This same process works with any sum of consecutive addends. To find the sum of an odd number of addends, simply take the middle number and multiply by the number of addends. For example $3 + 4 + 5 + 6 + 7 = 25$ or 5×5, since our middle addend is 5 and we have 5 addends. For an even number of addends, there is no middle number. The middle number is between two numbers in the set of addends. For example, with $7 + 8 + 9 + 10 = 34$, the middle number is 8.5. We multiply by the number of addends (4) and get our sum (34).

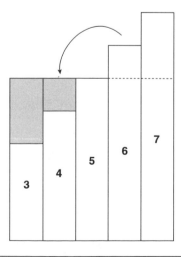

More on the Mathematics

Task
3

When investigating patterns, students may choose to look at strings of addends that all begin with the same addend. See the table below for the consecutive strings of consecutive addends which begin with 1.

Number of Addends	Sum
1	1
2	1+2=3
3	1+2+3=6
4	1+2+3+4=10
5	1+2+3+4+5=15
6	1+2+3+4+5+6=21
7	1+2+3+4+5+6+7=28
8	1+2+3+4+5+6+7+8=36

These sums are the triangular numbers.

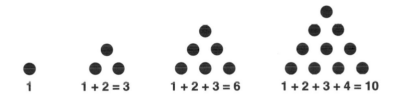

All such strings of consecutive addends, regardless of the value of the first addend (we could begin with 2 or 3 or 4, etc.), form *quadratic patterns*. A quadratic pattern is one in which the increase in value from one term in a series to the next increases at a constant rate. For example, the sums of strings of consecutive addends that begin with 1 form the following series: {1, 3, 6, 10, 15, 21, 28, 36...}. Taking the difference between each item in the series and the next, we arrive at the following series: {2, 3, 4, 5, 6, 7, 8...}. This occurs because these are the exact values that we had added to each string to get the subsequent string. These differences increase at a constant rate, by 1. For this reason, we have a quadratic pattern.

In the sample solution, we offered generalizations for sums of 2, 3, 4, and 5 consecutive addends. We can use Gauss's process and formula to determine the sum of any string of consecutive addends. Gauss noticed a shortcut method for adding these strings.

For example, consider:

$$3 + 4 + 5 + 6 + 7 + 8 + 9 + 10$$

Task

If we add the first and last addends, we get 13. We also get 13 by adding the second and second-to-the-last addends and so on:

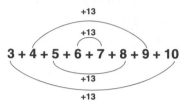

We get four 13s in all. We can then multiply 4×13 to get our sum. The 4 resulted from pairing addends together, so 4 is half the total number of addends.

We can use this process to derive a general formula for determining the sum of a string of consecutive addends that begins with 1. We have:

$$1 + 2 + 3 + 4 + ... + (n - 1) + n$$

We add the first and last addends and get $n + 1$. We add the second and second-to-the-last addends and also get $n + 1$ and so on:

$$1 + 2 + 3 + ... + (n - 2) + (n - 1) + n$$

The number of $(n + 1)$s is the same as the number of pairs of addends. Since we have n addends, we have $\frac{n}{2}$ pairs of addends. We then multiply $(n + 1)$ by $\frac{n}{2}$ to arrive at our sum: $\frac{n(n+1)}{2}$.

With this formula, we can generalize from our previous generalizations for the sums of 2 addends, 3 addends, 4 addends, and 5 addends: $2r + 3$, $3r + 6$, $4r + 10$, and $5r + 15$, where r is the value of the first addend minus 1. Remember that the numbers 3, 6, 10, and 15 are the sums resulting from adding the strings of consecutive addends that start with 1. Three is the sum of the first 2 consecutive addends, 6 the sum of the first 3 consecutive addends, and so on. Therefore, for n consecutive addends that begin with $(r + 1)$—(that is, if 5 is our first addend, the value for r is 4)—we can express the sum as follows: $nr + \frac{n(n+1)}{2}$.

Perhaps the following table will make this generalization clearer:

(r = the value of the first addend minus 1)

# of Addends	Sum
2	$2r + 3$
3	$3r + 6$
4	$4r + 10$
5	$5r + 15$
6	$6r + 21$
n	$nr + \dfrac{n(n+1)}{2}$

Remember that r and n are integers, $r \geq 0$ since our smallest addend is 1 and $n \geq 2$ because we always add at least two addends.

Why don't the powers of 2 work?

This task raises an interesting question: Why can't any of the powers of 2 be expressed as the sum of consecutive addends? Think about the structure of the powers of two and the structure of numbers that are sums of consecutive addends.

Notice that the powers of two are the only numbers whose prime factorization includes only the even prime (that is, nothing but 2s). The following argument shows that sums of consecutive addends must always have an odd factor.

We showed how all sums of consecutive addends can be expressed as:

$$nr + \frac{n(n+1)}{2}$$

where n is the number of addends and r is one less than the first addend in the string. The value for n can either be odd or even, depending on whether there is an even or odd number of consecutive addends. We can rewrite the above expression as:

$$n \frac{(2r+n+1)}{2}$$

since:

$$nr + \frac{n(n+1)}{2} = \frac{2nr}{2} + \frac{n(n+1)}{2}$$

$$= \frac{2nr + n(n+1)}{2}$$

$$= n \frac{(2r+n+1)}{2}$$

Task

If n is odd, we see how the sum must have an odd factor, namely n. To see what happens when n is even, we again rewrite the expression as follows:

$$\frac{n}{2}\,(2r+n+1)$$

If n is even, $\frac{n}{2}$ can be either even or odd. If $\frac{n}{2}$ is odd, then our sum has an odd factor. However if $\frac{n}{2}$ is even, then we must look at $(2r+n+1)$ for an odd factor. Regardless of whether r is even or odd, $2r$ must be even. Since here n is even, $2r+n$ must also be even, the sum of two even numbers. Adding 1 would give us an odd number. Therefore, $(2r+n+1)$ is an odd number, giving our sum an odd factor.

Using this Task

The launch is intended to familiarize students with the context of the task. Read through the first example in the *As a class* part of the task. You may want to ask your class what they think the word *consecutive* means. If no one knows, ask the students to look at the three examples of numbers that add up to 15 and to look at the numbers that are being added in each of those examples. Ask them to describe the numbers. If no one comes up with the fact that the numbers are "in order," then you may have to add that to the conversation. You can then tell the students that numbers that come in order are called *consecutive*. When you think your students understand *consecutive*, move on to the next example and explore a few examples of other numbers that can or cannot be written as sums of consecutive addends.

Once you feel that they understand the context of the problem, read with students the aims of the assessment in the box at the top of page 41. Have students work individually on the task. Make sure that students have access to as much paper as they need.

Issues for Classroom Use

This task involves some very rich mathematics. Students investigate numbers that can be written as a sum of consecutive positive integers. The task suggests that students begin their investigation by looking at numbers up to 36. This should be sufficient to notice numerous patterns. Students in rich curricular environments are generally successful at both noticing and generalizing about the patterns. After finding patterns, questions like these may arise: Do these patterns hold for all positive whole numbers? How do we know? Can we be sure? Can we prove it? For this assessment, students are not expected to make specific statements about patterns holding for all numbers or to prove that they do; these are, however, very interesting and provocative questions, which students may wish to explore. After completing the assessment, a teacher may wish to continue having students expand upon their findings and search for proof, either in class or on their own.

Characterizing Performance

This section offers a characterization of student responses and provides indications of the ways in which the students were successful or unsuccessful in engaging with and completing the task. The descriptions are keyed to the *Core Elements of Performance*. Our global descriptions of student work range from "The student needs significant instruction" to "The student's work meets the essential demands of the task." Samples of student work that exemplify these descriptions of performance are included below, accompanied by commentary on central aspects of each student's response. These sample responses are *representative*; they may not mirror the global description of performance in all respects, being weaker in some and stronger in others.

The characterization of student responses for this task is based on these *Core Elements of Performance:*

1. Systematically investigate consecutive addends.
2. Find patterns about which numbers can be expressed as sums of different numbers of consecutive addends.
3. Formulate generalizations about the patterns, using symbolic or natural language.
4. Hypothesize about why these patterns occur.

Descriptions of Student Work

The student needs significant instruction.

The student understands what consecutive addends are, evidenced by noting which numbers can or cannot be expressed as a sum of consecutive addends. However, the list of numbers may be small (no more than 10) and may be listed unsystematically. Student may attempt to describe patterns, but they are inadequate (unclear or incomplete).

Student A

The work of Student A indicates that she understands what consecutive addends are as evidenced by the incomplete paper listing the numbers 1 to 36 and her attempt to identify patterns within the context of the task. Although Student A is able to list some numbers and sets of consecutive addends, she does not adequately identify what the patterns are, nor does she attempt to establish patterns exhaustively. For example, she writes "they are all the odd #'s," outlining the pattern clearly, yet she does not use this pattern to find additional values for her chart.

The student needs some instruction.

Student systematically records all numbers 1 to 36 and notes which can or cannot be expressed as consecutive addends (list may be somewhat incomplete) OR student has systematically considered subsets of numbers that could potentially provide insights into patterns (for example, student looks at all the different consecutive addends that start with 1, or notices that the powers of 2 have no consecutive addend to represent them and checks by completing the set). The student may attempt to describe patterns, but the descriptions are inadequate (unclear or incomplete).

Student B

Student B systematically records the numbers investigated and records and describes one pattern, that of three consecutive addends. Other than this, the student fails to adequately identify and describe any patterns relating to the sums of consecutive addends. Student B does note the numbers 2, 4, 8, 16, and 32 and describes a relationship among these numbers ("these numbers double from the one before"), while not explicitly identifying this pattern as the pattern of numbers that cannot be written as the sum of consecutive addends.

The student's work needs to be revised.

The student has systematically recorded the investigation, and has identified at least three patterns (for example, sums of two addends are odd; sums of three addends are multiples of 3; there are no examples of sums that are powers of 2).

Student C

Student C correctly lists all the ways that the numbers up to 23 can be written as sums of consecutive addends. He correctly identifies three patterns (although the statement about four consecutive addends is off the mark). While Student C's statements about several of his patterns are correct, he does not completely identify the patterns. Had Student C generalized the patterns, it would have been a response that adequately meets the essential demands of the task (for example, for sums of three consecutive addends, you multiply the first addend by 3 and then add 6).

Task

The student's work meets the essential demands of the task.

The student has identified at least three patterns (for example, sums of two addends are odd; sums of three addends are multiples of 3; there are no examples of sums that are powers of 2), reasonably attempts to generalize descriptions for at least one of the patterns (either verbally or symbolically), and attempts to provide a reasoned explanation for at least one of the patterns (a verbal or symbolic "proof").

Student D

Student D conducts her investigation very systematically. In spite of occasional errors in her chart, she uses her evidence to adequately describe five patterns. Furthermore, Student D attempts to generalize about all the patterns she finds (see "Overall Patterns") and makes predictions of additional values that cannot be expressed as the sum of consecutive addends based on her generalization of this pattern. Student D attempts to explain why some of the patterns occur, albeit not completely. For example, she tries to explain why even numbers such as 30 cannot be written as the sum of two consecutive addends. She attempts to explain why the sums of four consecutive addends increase by 4: "First # of 4 addends is one more than previous. So is the last addend."

STAR QUALITY: Student successfully provides generalized proof for why powers of 2 cannot be represented by consecutive addends.

1 =

2 =

3 = 1+2

4 =

5 = 2+3

6 = 1+2+3

7 = 3+4

8 =

9 = 4+5 / 2+3+4

10 = 1+2+3+4

11 = 5+6

12 = 3+4+5

13 = 6+7

14 =

15 = 1+2+3+4+5 / 4+5+6 / 7+8

16 =

17 =

18 =

19 =

20 =

21 =

22 =

23 =

24 =

25 =

26 =

27 =

28 =

29 =

30 =

31 =

32 =

33 =

34 =

35 =

36 =

The First Number in the pattern is #6 the next Number is #9 and the next one after that is #15.

#3 is 1+2
#9 is 2+3+4/4+5
#15 is 4+5+6/7+8/1+2+3+4+5
also three is A Factor of All of the #'s ③x1 =3
③x3 =9   ③x5 =15
another pattern is #3, #6, #10, #15...

Not sure

#3 = 1+2
#6 = 1+2+3
#10 = 1+2+3+4
#15 = 1+2+3+4+5
another pattern is in #3, #5, #7, #9
#11, #15
#3 = 1+2
#5 = 2+3
#7 = 3+4
#9 = 4+5
#11 = 5+6
#15 = 6+7
also they are All the odd #'s.

Consecutive Addends ■ Student Work

Student B

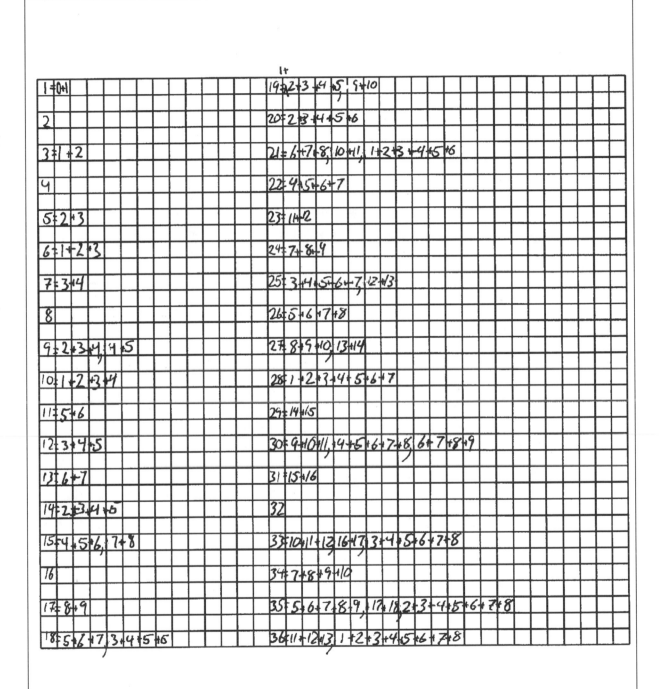

1=0+1

2

3=1+2

4

5=2+3

6=1+2+3

7=3+4

8

9=2+3+4, 4+5

10=1+2+3+4

11=5+6

12=3+4+5

13=6+7

14=2+3+4+5

15=4+5+6, 7+8

16

17=8+9

18=5+6+7, 3+4+5+6

1+

19=2+3+4+5, 9+10

20=2+3+4+5+6

21=6+7+8, 10+11, 1+2+3+4+5+6

22=4+5+6+7

23=11+2

24=7+8+9

25=3+4+5+6+7, 12+13

26=5+6+7+8

27=8+9+10, 13+14

28=1+2+3+4+5+6+7

29=14+15

30=9+10+11, 4+5+6+7+8, 6+7+8+9

31=15+16

32

33=10+11+12, 16+17, 3+4+5+6+7+8

34=7+8+9+10

35=5+6+7+8+9, 17+18, 2+3+4+5+6+7+8

36=11+12+13, 1+2+3+4+5+6+7+8

Starting from 1 (0+1) and going to 36 (11+12+13) each third number 1,3,6,9 ect. uses similar numbers to the number 3 before it. 1 is 0+1, 3 is 1+2, 6 is 1+2+3, 9 is 2+3+4. For each number that is added to the end (0+1 and 1+2, no more zero) the first number is taken away. There is no pattern for every fourth number. It has no answers for 4 or 8 but there is for 12 not one for 16 but there is one for 20. There is one for 24 and 28 but there is not one for 32. And lastly, there is one for 36. As you can see it is completly random. For the numbers 2,4,8,16 and 32 there is no pattern except that ~~there~~ the numbers dobble from the one before it.

1— 0 +1
2—
3— 1+2
4—
5— 2+3
6— 1+2+3
7— 3+4
9—
9— 4+5, — 2+3+4
10— 1+2+3+4
11— 5+6
12— 3+4+5
13— 6+7
14— 2+3+4+5
15— on front
16 —

17— 8+9
18— 3+4+5+6 5+6+7
19— 9+10
20 = 2+3+4+5+6

21— 10+11, 1+2+3+4+5, 6+7+8
22— 4+5+6+7
23— 11+12,

2) The numbers that can be written as two consecutive numbers are odd numbers.

The numbers that can be written as three consecutive numbers are multiples of 3.

The numbers that can be written as four consecutive numbers are multiples of 4.

The numbers that can be written as five consecutive numbers are multiples of 5.

3) The numbers that cannot have a consecutive number are numbers that increase by the previous number without consecutive number times two.

4) I noticed that the numbers that have consecutive numbers are multiples of the number of consecutive numbers.

Student D

	CONSEC	TWO #'s	THREE'S	Four #'s	Five #'s	SiX #'s
1	X	0+1				
2						
3	X	1+2				
4						
5	X	2+3				
6	X		1+2+3			
7	X	3+4				
8						
9	X	4+5	2+3+4			
10	X			1+2+3+4		
11	X	5+6				
12	X		3+4+5			
13	X	6+7				
14	X			2+3+4,5		
15	X	7+8	4+5+6		1+2+3+4+5	
16						
17	X	8+9				
18	X		5+6+7	3+4+5+6		
19	X	9+10				
20					2+3+4+5+6	
21	X	10+11	6+7+8			1+2+3+4+5+6
22	XX			4+5+6+7		
23	XX	11+12				
24	X		7+8+9			
25	X	12+13			3+4+5+6+7	

Conscc	Two #'s	THRee #'s	Four #'s	Five #'s	SiX #'s
26 X			5+6+7+8		
27 X	13+14	8+9+10			
28					1+2+3+4+5+6+7
29 X	14+15				↓
30 X		9+6+11	6+7+8+9	4+5+6+7+8	___
31 X	15+16				
32					3+4+5+6+7+8
33 X	16+17	10+11+12			↓
34 X			7+8+9+10		___
35 X	17+18			5+6+7+8+9	
36 X		11+12+13			
	18+19				4+5+6+7+8

To 64

The onLy #'s that Dont
Have any consezutiue ADDENDS
Are even #'s that couLDNT
Have CoNseCUTiUE ADDENs BECAUSE
OF THeiR PosiTion EX. #30
29 = 14 + 15
30 = EiTHER 15+15 or 16+14
31 = 15+6
NEither ARE ConseCuTiUe
FoR 30.

Numbers That Dont Have

consecutive ADDENDS ARE.
2, 4, 8, 16, 32, , 64 , .   128, 256 .....

paTTERN: Numbers w/out C. ADDens
DouBle iN value.

→ ⌐Two #'s⌐ PATTERN- ALL ODD
NUMBERS, NO EVEN NUMBERS.

→ ⌐THREE #'s PATTERN-STARTS AT
b. OCCURS AT:
        6, 9, 12, 15, 18, 21, ...
        EVERY THIRD #
6 = 1+2+3   FIRST OF THREE is
9 = 2+3+4   ONE MORE THAN PREVIOUS
12 = 3+4+5
15 = 4+5+6
18 = 5+6+7

→ ⌐FOUR #'s PATTERN-STARTS At 10
        EVERY FOURTH NUMBER
        ALL EVEN NUMBERS.
        OCCURS AT: 10, 14, 18, 22, 26 .....
10 = 1+2+3+4   18 = 3+4+5+6
14 = 2+3+4+5   22 = 4+5+6+7

Student D

FIRST # OF 4 ADDENDS
IS ONE MORE THAN
PREVIOUS SO IS THE Last
ADDEND.

→ ⌐————— FIVE #'s PATERN - STARTS
         AT 15
      OCCURS AT:
   15, 20, 25, 30, 35

   INCREASES BY FIVE

OVERALL PATTERNS

TWO# PATTERS EVERY SECOND #.
THREE # PATT. EVERY THIRD #.
FOUR # PATT. EVERY FOURTH #.
FIVE # PATT. EVERY FIFTH #.

• SO FOR TWO-FIVE & PATTERNS FOR #'s 1-36 EACH TIME THE NUMBERS OF ADDENDS INCREASES BY ONE, THE NUMBER BETWEEN OCCURANCES INCREASES BY ONE

• THE REASON 2, 4, 8, 16, 32 DON'T HAVE CONSECUTIVE ADDENDS ON THE TABLE IS BECAUSE NEGATIVE #'S WERE NOT USED THE PATTERNS ON THE TABLE WOULD CONTINUE IF THE NUMBERS BEZ ÷ME NEGATIVE.

THE #'s w/out CONSEC ADDENDS DouBLED

2,4,8,16,32

Emergency 911! Bay City

Choose appropriate statistical tools to analyze data.

Interpret statistics and graphs.

Make a recommendation based on analysis.

Long Task

Task Description

The task asks students to compare two ambulance companies on the basis of their timely response to Emergency 911 dispatches. Students must use appropriate graphs and/or measures of center and spread to present a persuasive argument for choosing one of the ambulance companies over the other.

Assumed Mathematical Background

It is assumed that students have had some experiences with situations that involve selecting appropriate variables to sort data, to represent data in tabular and graphical forms, and to find measures of center and spread. Further, it is assumed that students will have had experiences drawing conclusions and making recommendations based on data analysis.

Core Elements of Performance

- select appropriate methods for analyzing a data set including appropriate calculations and/or graphs
- select appropriate variables for sorting data
- construct, read, and interpret graphs
- make a policy recommendation and give clear reasons to justify that decision

Circumstances

Grouping:	Students may discuss the task in pairs and complete a combined written response.
Materials:	graph paper
Estimated time:	60 minutes

Emergency 911! Bay City

This problem gives you the chance to

- *select appropriate methods to analyze a data set, including appropriate graphs and calculations*
- *read and interpret a graph*
- *use data analysis to make recommendations*

With a partner

Last week there was an accident at the Waterfront Amusement Park in Bay City. A seat on one of the rides broke loose, resulting in the deaths of two teenagers. The owners of the amusement park have charged that if ambulances had responded more quickly, the two teens would have survived. They have threatened to sue the Bay City 911 emergency service for failing to dispatch ambulances efficiently.

The Bay City Council has hired your firm to conduct an independent investigation of the city's 911 response. Upon completion of your investigation, you are to make a report to the City Council on your findings, along with any recommendations for improving the Bay City 911 emergency service.

Your investigation has uncovered the following information.

- The 911 operators dispatch ambulances from two companies: Arrow Ambulance Service and Metro Ambulances.
- The 911 operators aren't always sure which company to send when an emergency call is received.
- Data on the response times of the two companies for an area of a one-mile radius of the Amusement Park show that responses can take as little as 6 minutes or as long as 19 minutes. (The response time is the length of time from when a 911 operator receives an emergency call to when an ambulance arrives at the scene of the accident.)

You need to continue your investigation by analyzing the response time data from the 911 log sheets for May. (The log sheets are shown on the next page.)

Based on the information above and on your analysis of the response time data, you conclude that the Bay City Council needs to establish a policy about which service to call.

Write a report to the Bay City Council advising them of your recommendations about how the 911 operators should make dispatches in the area around the amusement park.

You will need to prepare charts, graphs, calculations, or other materials to support your recommendations.

Be sure to give clear reasons for the policy you are recommending.

Emergency 911 data sheet

These log sheets show all the emergency calls placed to 911 operators in
May for an area within a one-mile radius of the Waterfront Amusement Park.

Date of call	Time of call	Company name	Response time in minutes
Wed., May 1	2:20 A.M.	Arrow	11
Wed., May 1	12:41 P.M.	Arrow	8
Wed., May 1	2:29 P.M.	Metro	11
Thurs., May 2	8:14 A.M.	Metro	8
Thurs., May 2	6:23 P.M.	Metro	16
Fri., May 3	4:15 A.M.	Metro	7
Fri., May 3	8:41 A.M.	Arrow	19
Sat., May 4	7:12 A.M.	Metro	11
Sat., May 4	7:43 P.M.	Metro	11
Sat., May 4	10:02 P.M.	Arrow	7
Sun., May 5	12:22 P.M.	Metro	12
Mon., May 6	6:47 A.M.	Metro	9
Mon., May 6	7:15 A.M.	Arrow	16
Mon., May 6	6:10 P.M.	Arrow	8
Tues., May 7	5:37 P.M.	Metro	16
Tues., May 7	9:37 P.M.	Metro	11
Thurs., May 9	5:30 A.M.	Arrow	17
Thurs., May 9	6:18 P.M.	Arrow	6
Fri., May 10	6:25 A.M.	Arrow	16
Sat., May 11	1:03 A.M.	Metro	12
Mon., May 13	6:40 A.M.	Arrow	17
Mon., May 13	3:25 P.M.	Metro	15
Tues., May 14	4:59 P.M.	Metro	14
Thurs., May 16	10:11 A.M.	Metro	8
Thurs., May 16	11:45 A.M.	Metro	10
Fri., May 17	11:09 A.M.	Arrow	7
Fri., May 17	9:15 P.M.	Arrow	8
Fri., May 17	11:15 P.M.	Metro	8
Mon., May 20	7:25 A.M.	Arrow	17
Mon., May 20	4:20 P.M.	Metro	19
Thurs., May 23	2:39 P.M.	Arrow	10
Thurs., May 23	3:44 P.M.	Metro	14
Fri., May 24	8:56 P.M.	Metro	10
Sat., May 25	8:30 P.M.	Arrow	8
Sun., May 26	6:33 A.M.	Metro	6
Mon., May 27	4:21 P.M.	Arrow	9
Tues., May 28	8:07 A.M.	Arrow	15
Tues., May 28	5:02 P.M.	Arrow	7
Wed., May 29	10:51 A.M.	Metro	9
Wed., May 29	5:11 P.M.	Metro	18
Thurs., May 30	4:16 A.M.	Arrow	10
Fri., May 31	8:59 A.M.	Metro	11

A Sample Solution

Calculating the mean response times for each ambulance service is a reasonable start to analyzing the data. However, the mean response time for Arrow Ambulance Service is 11.36 minutes and the mean response time for Metro Ambulances is 11.56 minutes. The difference of 0.2 minute is not significant and suggests that some further investigation of the data is warranted.

A likely choice for arranging the data would be to select response time and time of call to see if there is a relationship between these variables. A scatter plot graphing the response times for given times at which the calls were placed is an appropriate graphical representation.

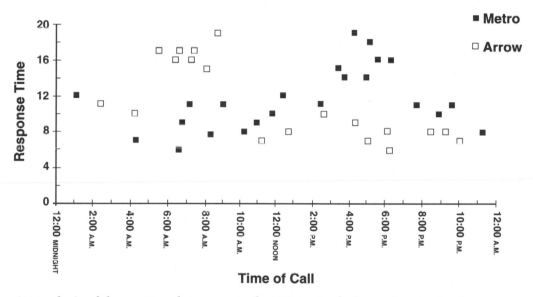

An analysis of the scatter plot suggests that Metro Ambulance Service tends to have a quicker response time during the A.M. hours and Arrow Ambulance Service tends to have a quicker response time during the P.M. hours. Given this analysis, a reasonable policy recommendation would be to have 911 operators dispatch Metro Ambulances between the morning hours from 12 midnight until 12 noon and to dispatch Arrow Ambulance Service during the afternoon and evening hours from 12 noon until 12 midnight.

A more complete solution would take into account whether there might be other relationships that affect a policy recommendation. Further analysis of the data could consider the relationship between response time and the day of the week in which a call is recorded. A scatter plot of these data is presented next.

Task

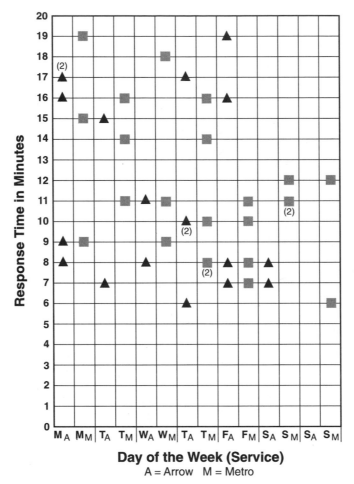

An analysis of this scatter plot suggests that the day of the week in which a call is received by a 911 operator has no effect on the response time.

Using this Task

Read through the task with students, making sure they understand the context of the task. You may want to ask some of the following questions to check their understanding.

> What is a 911 service?
> Could someone explain what a log sheet is?
> What do the data in the log sheet represent?
> What does it mean in the problem when it refers to "response time"?

After you are sure that students understand the context and what they are to do, leave them to their work. DO NOT give hints on how to analyze the data; students are to choose their own methods.

Issues for Classroom Use

To be able to tackle this task, students in the middle grades will need to have had some experiences with situations that involve selecting appropriate variables to sort data. We have found that without this kind of experience, students do not make much progress beyond simply calculating the mean response times, or they construct graphs that are not reasonable (for example, circle graphs) or informative, or construct graphs using variables that are not salient.

Task

Characterizing Performance

This section offers a characterization of student responses and provides indications of the ways in which the students were successful or unsuccessful in engaging with and completing the task. The descriptions are keyed to the *Core Elements of Performance*. Our global descriptions of student work range from "The student needs significant instruction" to "The student's work meets the essential demands of the task." Samples of student work that exemplify these descriptions of performance are included below, accompanied by commentary on central aspects of each student's response. These sample responses are *representative;* they may not mirror the global description of performance in all respects, being weaker in some and stronger in others.

The characterization of student responses for this task is based on these *Core Elements of Performance:*

1. Select appropriate methods for analyzing a data set including appropriate calculations and/or graphs.
2. Select appropriate variables for sorting data.
3. Construct, read, and interpret graphs.
4. Make a policy recommendation and give clear reasons to justify that decision.

Descriptions of Student Work

The group needs significant instruction.

Groups calculate a single statistic (for example, mean or median response time). They recommend one ambulance service over the other on the basis of a comparison of this single statistic, even though the mean difference is only 0.2 minutes, not significant for making a policy recommendation. The analysis of the data ignores all other variables except response time.

Group A

This group calculates the mean response time for Metro and Arrow ambulance services and then recommends that Metro is the best choice because their response time (incorrectly calculated) is 0.35 minutes quicker. The presentation of a bar graph of the mean response times adds nothing to the persuasiveness of their argument.

The group needs some instruction.

Groups may calculate measures of center and explore the data with other kinds of analysis (for example, box plots, stem-and-leaf plots) but they consider only a single variable—the response times of the two ambulance services. They demonstrate some ability to use their statistical "toolkit," but the analysis is not connected to the real-world context of the problem and the argument is weak.

Group B

This group restricts its analysis to a single variable—response time. They construct stem-and-leaf plots and box plots but use these displays to make a rather weak argument. They base their response on differences in the distribution of the response times, claiming that Arrow's times are more spread out. This group has not carefully and thoroughly interpreted the data, and their argument is not persuasive.

The group's work needs to be revised.

Groups select appropriate variables for analyzing the data (for example, response time in relation to time of call), make appropriate calculations, use appropriate graphical representations, and make a reasonable recommendation based on their analysis. There may be errors in the calculations and in the graphs. However, these groups do not fully analyze the data set, thereby not ruling out other possible salient relationships (for example, mean response time in relation to day of the call). The recommendations follow from the analysis but the report may lack clarity and thoroughness.

Group C

This group has selected the response time and the time of the call and have used a scatter plot to represent their analysis. Their recommendation is reasonable given the way in which they have analyzed the data. However, they have not pursued any other relationships among the variables in the data set.

The group's work meets the essential demands of the task.

Groups select appropriate variables for sorting, analyzing, and representing the data. These groups consider a number of relationships and use a variety of analytic tools to fully interrogate the data set. Their recommendations follow from and are supported by their analysis of the data.

Task

4

Group D

This group first considered the relationship between the response time and the time of the call, and they drew a broken line graph. Although it is not appropriate to connect the points on this graph given the context of the problem, they have presented a visually powerful representation of the data that supports a recommendation to use Metro in the A.M. and Arrow in the P.M. However, this group went on to examine the data further. They drew from their statistical toolkit, constructing a box plot, line plot, 5-number summary, and individual graphs for each ambulance service, but they concluded that this further analysis did not add anything new to their original analysis.

Group E

This group analyzed two relationships—response time to time of the call, and response time to day of the call. They concluded that there was a relationship between time of call and response time and recommended that Metro be called in the A.M. and Arrow in the P.M. They also commented that the day of the week did not seem to have an effect on the response time. They have done a careful investigation of the data and have made recommendations that follow from and are supported by their analysis.

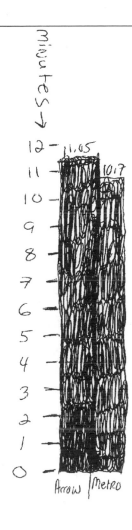

Arrow | Metro

Averages of minutes taken to respond to Accidents

✳ Report ✳

✳ Dear Bay City Council members,
As you know, the recent deaths of two teens at the Waterfront Ammusement park have caused the owners to file a lawsuit against the town's 911 service, and also raising the question of which ambulance company is the most efficient. The 911 service uses two different ambulance companies, Arrow and Metro, and among these two Metro has the fastest average response time and is used the most. Therefore I conclude that Metro is the best choice of ambulance service,

We recommend the Bay city council Metro ambulances for an emergency, because if you look at the graph you can see that the Metro's ambulances over all don't take as long as arrow ambulance service. Metro's median is higher then arrows, but Metro's data is more together then arrow. Arrows data is more spread out. If you call arrow's service you'll never know when they will get there. If you call Metro's service you have a better idea of when they're going to get there. So over all Metro's service is more eficient then Arrows service. Metro would be better to use.

Stem and leaf Plots

Respond
Time
(In minutes)

Metro

0	
a	
b	
c	7889
1	001111
a	22
b	445
c	66
d	9
e	

Arrow

0	
a	
b	6
c	77788889
1	001
a	
b	5
c	66777
d	9
e	

Key
0 = #'s 1-2
a = #'s 3-4
b = #'s 5-6
c = #'s 7-9
1 = #'s 10-11
a = #'s 12-13
b = #'s 14-15
c = #'s 16-17
d = #'s 18-19
e = #'s 20-21

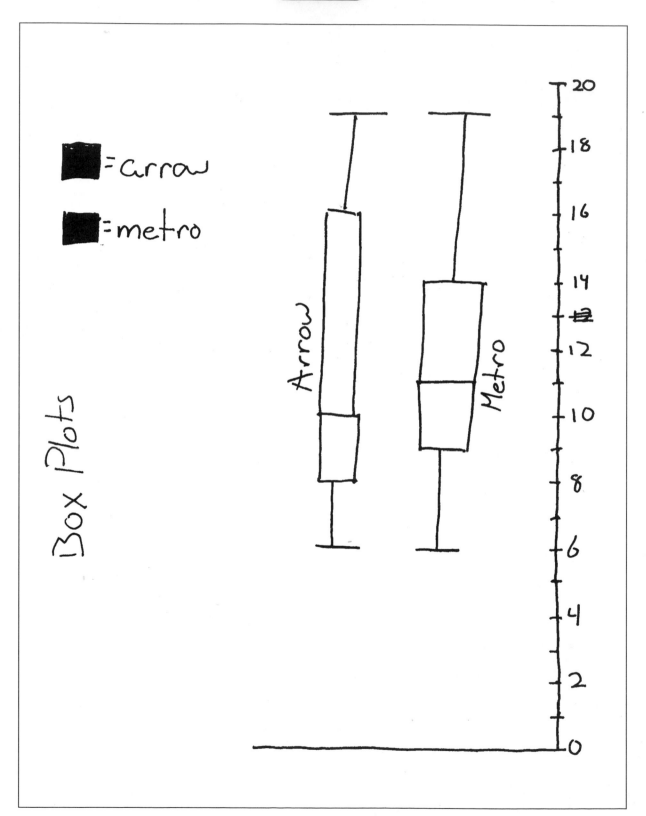

■ = arrow

■ = metro

Box Plots

Arrow

Metro

We conclude that metro should take all the calls from 12:00 Am to 12:00 p.m. and Arrow should take all the calls from 12:00 P.M. to 12:Am. If you look at the graph you can see that the plots are later, for ~~Arrow~~ from 12:00 Pm to 12:00 Am and earlier for Arrow. The plots are later, for metro from 12:00 Am → 12:00 pm and earlier for Arrow.

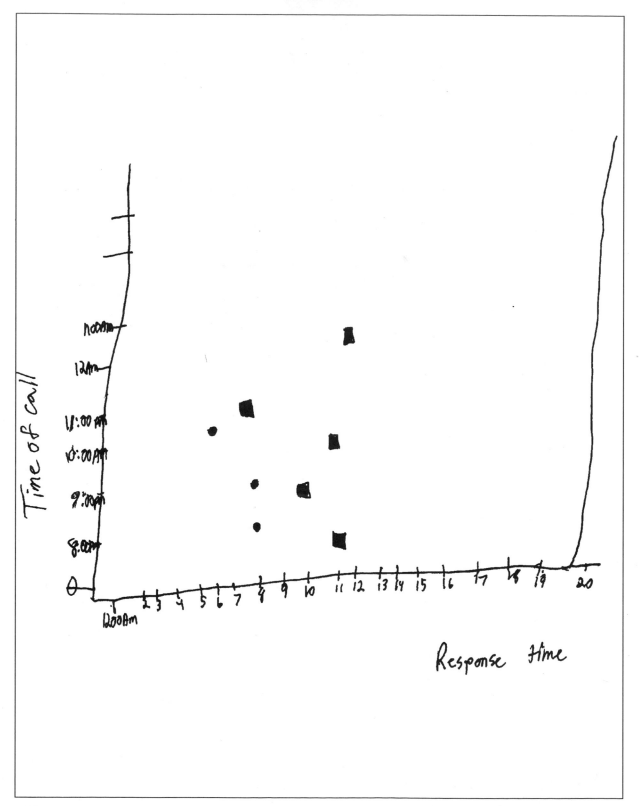

Group C

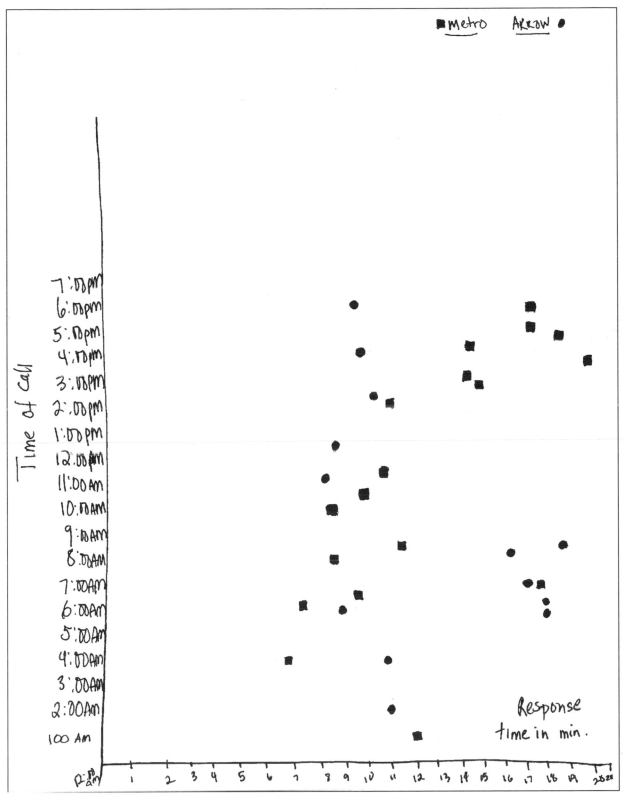

Our group reccommends that the Bay City Council hire the metro in the morning (midnight- noon ☀) and the arrow at night (noon-midnight 🌙)

This is because the metro has a better response time in the morning and the arrow had a faster time in the evening. You can tell by looking at the graph because the metro (blue) has a lower response time in the morning and the arrow had a lower response time in the evening. We also drew different graphs to express wich company we thought was the best such as # line plots, box plots, 5# summary, and we took the avreadge of the arrow and metro companies. But we found out that these graphs didn't help us find our answer.

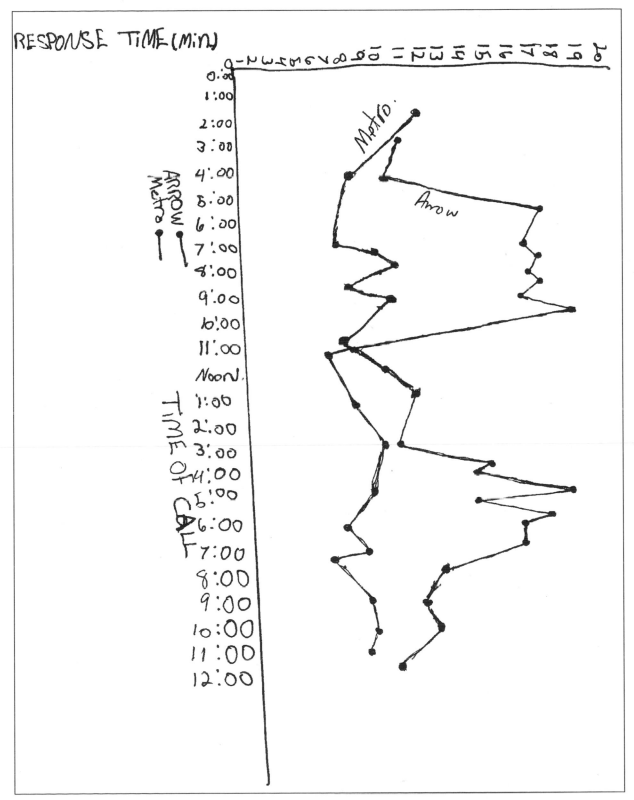

Group D

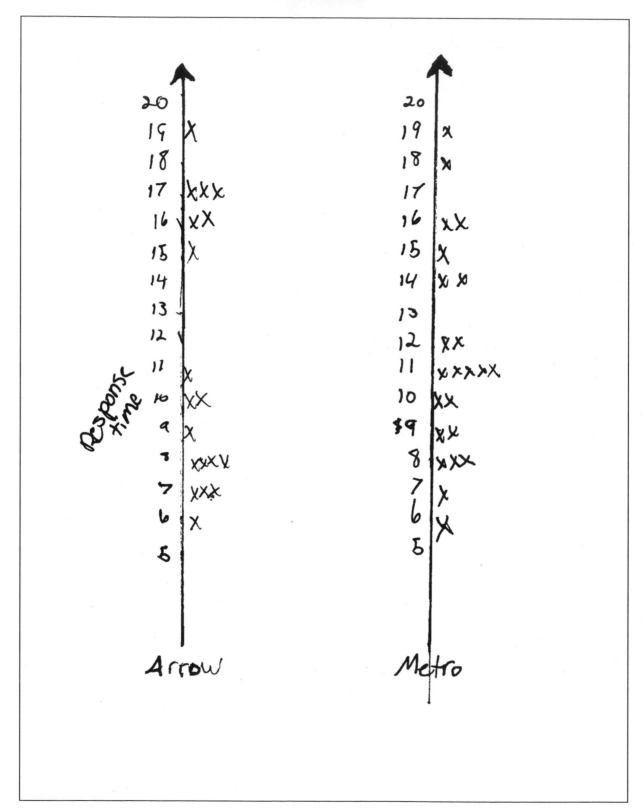

Group D

ARROW

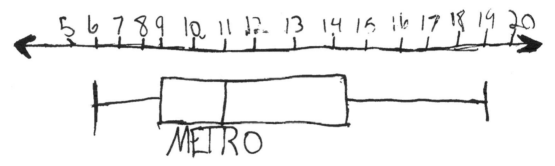

METRO

5 number summary:

Arrow	METRO	AVERAGE?	
min 6	min 6		
Q1-8	Q1-9	Arrow	Metro
med-9.5	Med-11	11.4	11.6
Q3-16	Q3-14	11.36	11.66
Max-19	Max-19		

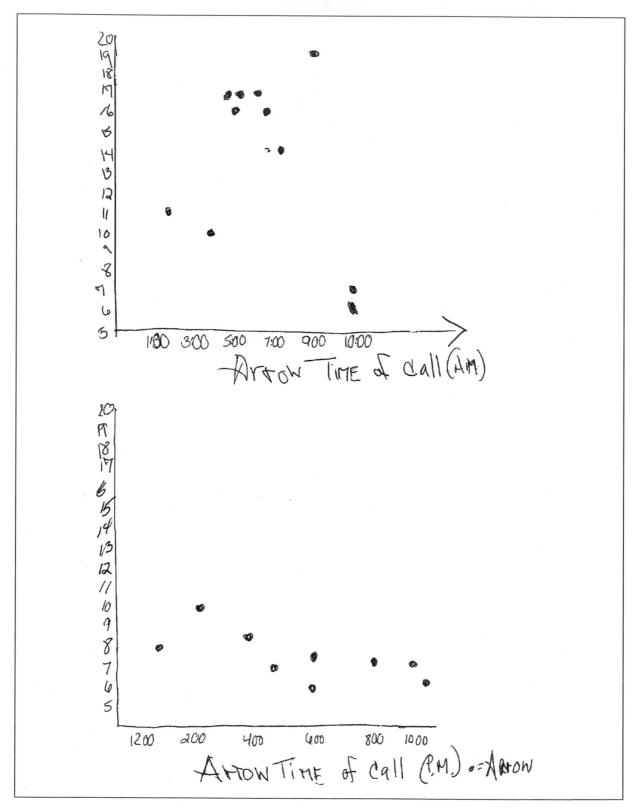

Group D

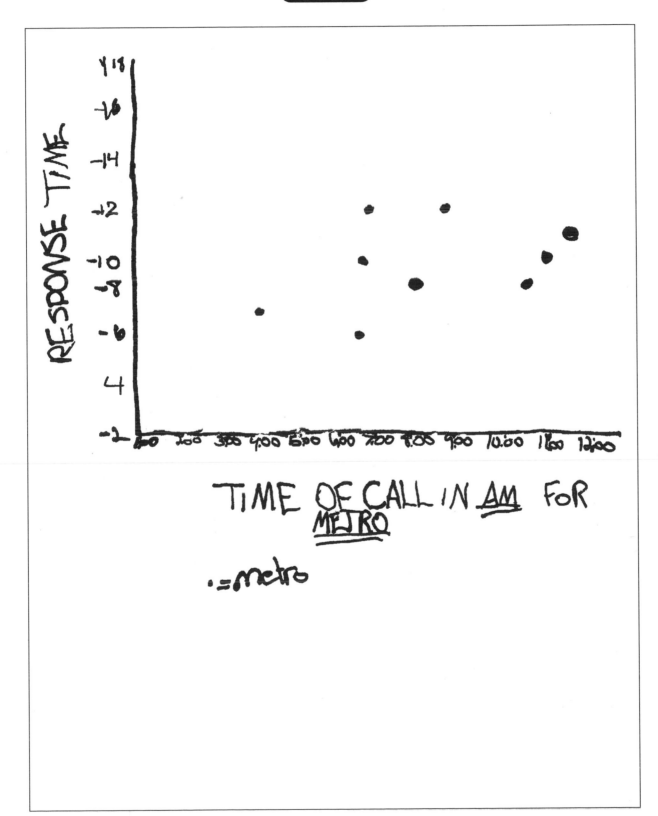

TIME OF CALL IN <u>AM</u> FOR <u>METRO</u>

•=metro

Group D

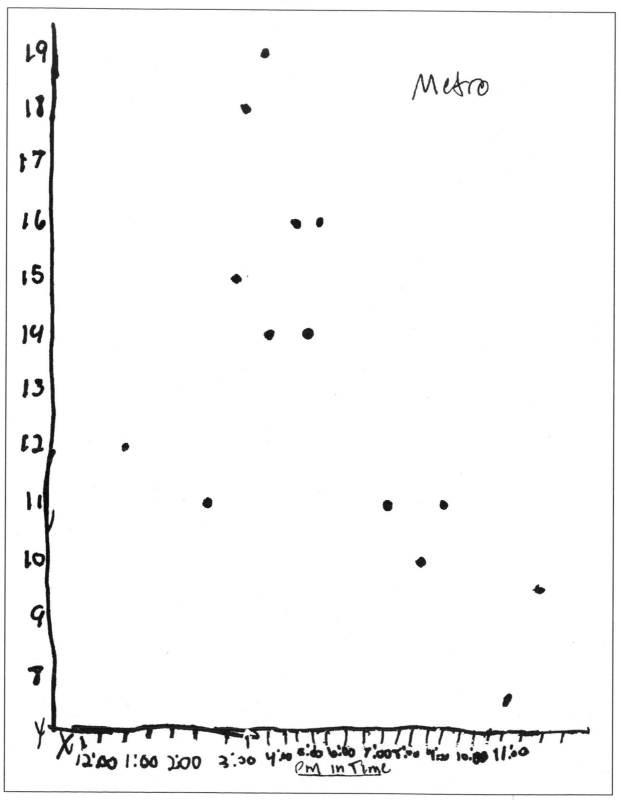

Council   Letter

Between 12:00 am. and 12:00 pm.
The Arrow Service has a higher
response time than the Metro does.
Between 12:00 pm and 12:00 am
the Metro has a higher response
time than the Arrow service.

If there was ever a call in
the am I would call the Metro
service and if there is ever a call
in the p.m I would call the
Arrow Service.

The different days of the week
does not effect the response time
by each service.

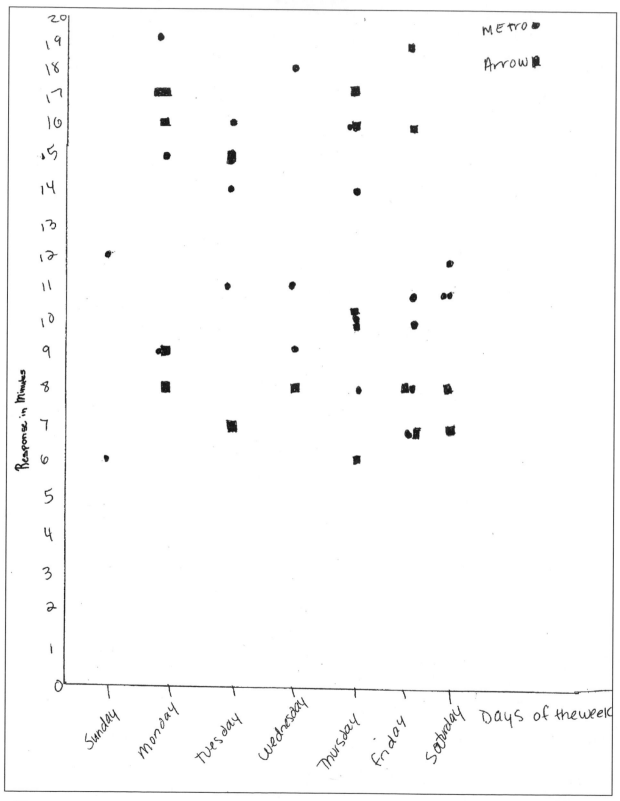

Student E

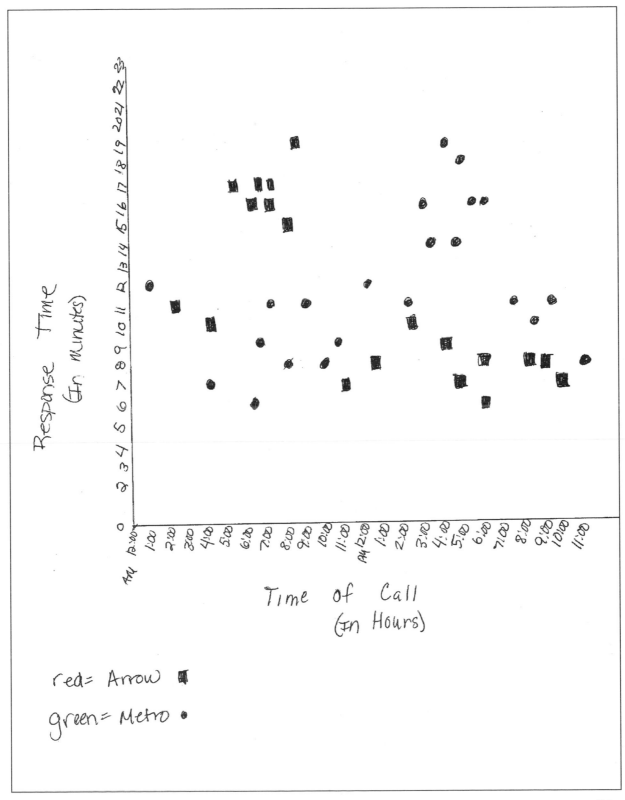

Response Time (In Minutes)

0 2 3 4 5 6 7 8 9 10 11 12 13 14 15 16 17 18 19 20 21 22 23

AM 12:00 1:00 2:00 3:00 4:00 5:00 6:00 7:00 8:00 9:00 10:00 11:00 PM 12:00 1:00 2:00 3:00 4:00 5:00 6:00 7:00 8:00 9:00 10:00 11:00

Time of Call
(In Hours)

red = Arrow ■
green = Metro ●

Sum of Seven

Long Task

Task Description

This task asks students to decide whether a dice game that first graders are using to practice their addition facts is a fair game. Students can use either theoretical or experimental probability to analyze this problem.

Assumed Mathematical Background

It is assumed that students have had experiences with finding experimental and theoretical probabilities.

Core Elements of Performance

- analyze and reason about probability
- design and implement a method for analyzing fairness
- make and justify a decision about the fairness of a game

Circumstances

Grouping:	Students complete an individual written response.
Materials:	dice, one pair per student
Estimated time:	30 minutes

Sum of Seven

This problem gives you the chance to

- *reason about probability*
- *design and use a method for evaluating fairness*
- *make and justify a decision*

On your own

The first-grade teacher wants Keisha and Shawna to practice their addition facts. To make this more interesting, the teacher has created a game. The students play the game by rolling a pair of dice and finding the sum of the numbers rolled. It is okay for Keisha and Shawna to help each other find the sums.

Points are awarded in the following manner:

     If the sum is seven, then Keisha gets 7 points.

     If the sum is *not* seven, then Shawna gets 1 point.

Decide if the game is fair or not and give reasons for your answer.

_____

_____

_____

_____

A Sample Solution

Method A: (Theoretical)

Table of Sums

		First Die					
		1	2	3	4	5	6
Second Die	1	2	3	4	5	6	7
	2	3	4	5	6	7	8
	3	4	5	6	7	8	9
	4	5	6	7	8	9	10
	5	6	7	8	9	10	11
	6	7	8	9	10	11	12

Keisha's probability of getting a 7 is $\frac{6}{36}$. In theory, she can expect to get 6 "wins" in 36 rolls: She could expect 6×7 or 42 points.

Shawna's probability of not getting 7 is $\frac{30}{36}$. In theory Shawna can expect to get 30 "wins" out of 36 rolls. She could expect 30 points.

This game is unfair since Keisha and Shawna do not have the same expected number of points after a certain number of trials (in this case, 36 trials).

Task

Method B: (Experimental)
I'll roll the pair of dice 100 times and keep track of "7" and "not 7."

Keisha (7)	Shawna (not 7)
ЖГ ЖГ	ЖГ ЖГ ЖГ
ЖГ IIII	ЖГ ЖГ ЖГ
	ЖГ ЖГ ЖГ
	ЖГ ЖГ ЖГ
	ЖГ ЖГ ЖГ
	ЖГ I

19 "7"s = **133 points**   81 "not 7"s = **81 points**

This game looks like it favors Keisha. I did this like an experiment so my numbers are estimates of what will most likely happen if you play the game a lot of times. I believe I did plenty of tosses to feel confident about my results, and that the game will consistently favor Keisha no matter how many times I play. So, it is not a fair game.

Using this Task

Review with the students the aims of this assessment listed in the box at the top of the student activity page. Read the task with your students and make sure all students understand the context of the task. Let students show their strengths by pursuing the method of their choice. You may need to remind students that the first graders will roll the dice repeatedly or that the goal of the task is to determine whether or not the game is fair.

Issues for Classroom Use

Students may use either theoretical or experimental methods. A key element in the use of theoretical methods is developing an exhaustive list of possibilities. A key element in the use of experimental methods is to gather data on a reasonable set of trials. In this particular task, students should toss the dice at least 100 times.

A student may use both experimental and theoretical methods. If a student uses both methods without reconciling the results of the two methods (if the methods result in different outcomes), then it cannot be assumed that the student has a robust understanding of each method or the power of the theoretical over the experimental.

Task

Characterizing Performance

This section offers a characterization of student responses and provides indications of the ways in which the students were successful or unsuccessful in engaging with and completing the task. The descriptions are keyed to the *Core Elements of Performance.* Our global descriptions of student work range from "The student needs significant instruction" to "The student's work meets the essential demands of the task." Samples of student work that exemplify these descriptions of performance are included below, accompanied by commentary on central aspects of each student's response. These sample responses are *representative;* they may not mirror the global description of performance in all respects, being weaker in some and stronger in others.

The characterization of student responses for this task is based on these *Core Elements of Performance:*
1. Analyze and reason about probability.
2. Design and implement a method for analyzing fairness.
3. Make and justify a decision about the fairness of a game.
NOTE: Depending on whether students use theoretical or experimental probability, two important aspects are:
  Conducting a sufficient number of trials using experimental methods.
  Accounting for all possibilities using theoretical methods.

Descriptions of Student Work

The student needs significant instruction.

Student engages in some data or probability analysis, but the system or approach is incorrect or incoherent.

Student A

Student A does engage in some data analysis, but the method is seriously flawed: the rolls of the dice for which the sums are not equal to seven are not tallied. A correct conclusion is drawn about the fairness of the game but the argument is based on the number of events not equal to seven rather than the expected number of points.

The student needs some instruction.

Student begins with a potentially correct method of data or probability analysis, but the analysis may be incomplete (for example, too few trials for an experimental approach); conclusions drawn may be incorrect or based upon incomplete information. (For example, the student does not consider expected value of points won.)

Student B

Student B uses both theoretical and experimental methods but neither method is complete. Not enough trials are run for the experimental method to make a convincing case, especially since there is no evidence that the student has calculated the expected number of points. Not all outcomes are determined in the theoretical approach, so the expected number of points cannot be calculated. While a conclusion is drawn, there is no justification.

The student's work needs to be revised.

Student has implemented an analysis that is complete and indicates the expected number of points. However, the reasoning used for justification is flawed, vague, incomplete, or inconsistent with the results of the analysis.

Student C

Student C uses a theoretical method correctly, accounting for all possibilities and expected points. Although his justification is based on the findings from the analysis, there is a major flaw in reasoning. When Student C finds that Shawna is expected to get 30 points and Keisha is expected to get 42 points, the student then states that 30 and 42 are the most points Shawna and Keisha could get. This is incorrect because 30 and 42 would be expected to be the number of points for 36 trials of the game, not the maximum. In addition, the student shows a weak understanding of "fair" by stating that the game is "not fair for Shawna," but presumably *is* fair for Keisha.

The student's work meets the essential demands of the task.

Student has implemented an analysis that is complete and indicates the expected number of points. The reasoning used for justification is sound (based on using expectation and averages to predict situations under uncertainty) and is based on the findings of the data analysis.

Student D

Student D uses a theoretical method correctly and completely. The conclusion drawn is appropriately based on the results of the data analysis. The reasoning is sound.

Student A

getting 7
(IN #)
							= 105

On your own

The first grade teacher wants Keisha and Shawna to practice their addition facts. To make this more interesting, the teacher has created a game. The students play the game by rolling a pair of dice and finding the sum of the numbers rolled. It is okay for Keisha and Shawna to help each other find the sums.

Points are awarded in the following manner:

If the sum is seven, then Keisha gets 7 points.

If the sum is *not* seven, then Shawna gets 1 point.

Decide if the game is fair or not and give reasons for your answer.

UNFAIR — There is more of a chance not to get 7, It's easier to get other #'s, Because there are more #'s than 7.

Sum of 7

Experimental Prob

seven	other than Seven
~~THL THL~~	~~THL THL~~
~~THL THL~~	Keisha
~~THL THL~~	
~~THL~~	
Shana	

Theoretical Prob.

1,1	2,2	3,3	4,4	5,5	6,6
1,2	2,3	(3,4)	4,5	5,6	
1,3	2,4	3,5	4,6		
1,4	(2,5)	3,6			
1,5	2,6				
(1,6)					

The game is not fair Keisha would get more points according to my theoretical and expiremental probability.

Student C

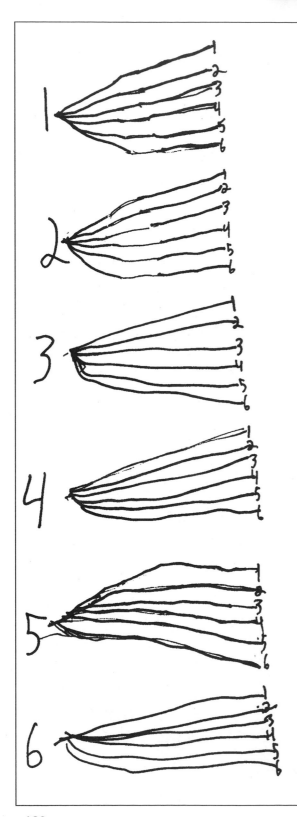

1
1-2
13
1-4
1-5
1-6
2-1
2-2
2-3
2-4
2-5
2-6
3-1
3-2
3-3
3-4
3-5
3-6

4-1
4-2
4-3
4-4
4-5
4-6

5-1
5-2
5-3
5-4
5-5
5-6
6-1
6-2
6-3
6-4
6-5
6-6

Student C

SUM OF SEVEN

Theoretically—The chance of rolling
7 is $\frac{6}{36}$ or $\frac{1}{6}$

The Chance of rolling any
Other number is $\frac{30}{36}$ or $\frac{5}{6}$

The game is not fair because
the most points Shawna could
get is 30 the most Keisha could
get is 42. It is not fair for Shawna.

Theoretical out comes
What the possible out comes can be

1,1 2,1 31 41 51 (61)
1,2 2,2 32 42 (52) 62
1,3 2,3 33 (43) 53 63
1,4 2,4 (34) 44 64 64
1,5 (2,5) 35 45 55 65
(1,6) 2,6 36 46 56 66

P=(keisha)=42 points
p=(Shawna)=30points

I got 42 points but there where 6
time 7 come up so I X 6X7 and got
42
I got 30 by count up all of the other
out come and got 30.

The game is not fair because Keisha
theoretically could get 12 more points
than Shawna

6

T-shirt Design

Long Task

Task Description

This task asks students to describe a geometric design for a T-shirt (that combines a circle and several segments on a grid) to a friend over the phone so that she/he can reproduce the design.

Assumed Mathematical Background

It is assumed that students have had experience with systems for locating points, lines, shapes, and circles on a grid. This task allows for nonconventional and invented systems to locate the design.

Core Elements of Performance

- locate the placement of all parts of the design (circle, diameter, zigzag) on a grid

- use an efficient and systematic approach (may be an invented system)

- give a clear set of directions

Circumstances

Grouping:	Following a class introduction, students complete an individual written response.
Materials:	compasses, rulers, and protractors or angle rulers may be requested
Estimated time:	30 minutes

T-shirt Design

The design below, including the 10-by-10 grid, is going to be used on a math team T-shirt. You accidentally took the original design home, and your friend Chris needs it tonight. Chris has no fax machine, but he does have a 10-by-10 grid just like yours (see Chris's grid on the next page). You must call Chris on the telephone and tell him very precisely how to draw the design on his grid.

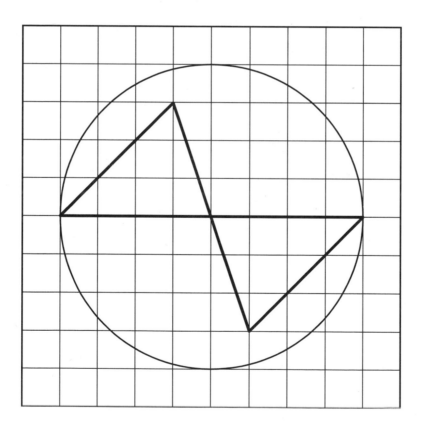

This problem gives you the chance to

- *systematically communicate about geometric shapes*
- *locate shapes on a grid*
- *give a clear set of directions*

On your own

This is the grid that Chris has in front of him. Prepare for your phone call by writing out your directions. Once you have finished, check your work to make sure that Chris will be able to recreate the design from your description.

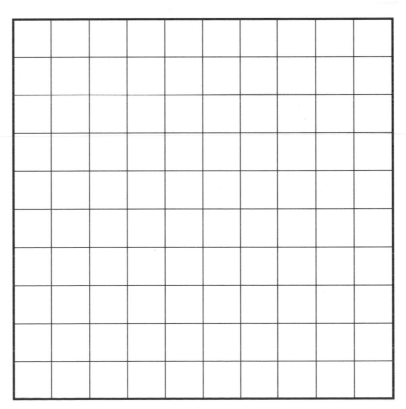

Task **A Sample Solution**

The following are four alternative sample solutions.

A. This solution uses an invented coordinate system similar to the Cartesian coordinate system.

Before you begin the drawing of the design, you need to label the 10-by-10 grid. Start in the upper-left-hand corner and label that first dark line "1." Then going across, number each of the lines until you get to 11. Now, do the same thing going down. Start with the upper left dark line and label that "1." Continue going down until you get to 11.

Now you can start drawing the design.

1. First draw a circle with a radius of 4 units and a center at the point where the 6 across and 6 down lines meet.
2. Now go to where the 2 across line and the 6 down line meet. Draw a straight line from this point over to the point where 10 across and 6 down meet. This line should go through the center of the circle.
3. Starting from the 2 across and 6 down point (from where you started the last line), draw a straight line to the point at 5 across, 3 down. Starting at 5 across, 3 down, draw a straight line to the point at 7 across and 9 down. Draw one more straight line from this last point to 10 across and 6 down.
4. The finished picture should look like a tilted bow tie inside a circle. If it looks like this, you are done.

B. The Cartesian coordinate (x, y) system is another system that students may use to describe the design.

Number the vertical lines from left to right along the bottom of your grid from 0 to 10. This is your x-axis. Then number the horizontal lines from bottom to top along the left side of your grid from 0 to 10. This is your y-axis. I will specify points by giving the x-value first and then the y-value.

Now you can start drawing the design.
1. Draw a circle with a radius of 4 units and a center at the point (5, 5).
2. Draw a line from the point (1, 5) to (9, 5). This is the diameter of the circle.
3. Draw a line from (1, 5) to (4, 8). Draw a line from (4, 8) to (6, 2). Then draw a line from (6, 2) to (9, 5).
4. Your picture should look like a tilted bow tie inside a circle. If it does, you are done.

C. Another system students may use involves numbering the boxes of the grid from 1 to 100.

Task

6

Begin by numbering across starting with 1 from the upper left hand corner. Once you have reached 10 and filled the first row of boxes, start the next row by numbering across left to right, from 11 to 20. Continue in this manner until you have filled all the boxes and reached 100.

1. Find the point where the boxes 41, 42, 51, and 52 meet.
2. Connect that point to the point where boxes 49, 50, 59, and 60 meet.
3. Starting at the point you found in Step 1, draw a line to the point where 14, 15, 24, and 25 meet.
4. Connect the point where boxes 14, 15, 24, and 25 meet to the point where boxes 76, 77, 86, and 87 meet.
5. Starting at the point where 76, 77, 86, and 87 meet, draw a straight line to the point where 49, 50, 59, and 60 meet.
6. Use a compass opened to 4 units (on the grid) to draw a circle around the two triangles putting the point of the compass where 45, 46, 55, and 56 meet.

D. Another system students may use involves the use of measuring tools with the grid.

1. Put the ruler on the middle line going across the box. This is the sixth line from the bottom (counting the bottom line as 1) and it is also the sixth line from the top of the box. Count in one unit from each side of the box, and draw a bold line that is 8 units across. There will be one unit that was not included on each end. Label the left end A and the right end B.
2. Using point A as a vertex and the line segment drawn in Step 1 as a side of an angle, measure a 45-degree angle "going up" from the segment drawn in Step 1. Draw a line segment along that angle that is about 4.5 units long. (It should cross diagonally through 3 squares.) Label the open end of that line segment C.
3. Using point B as a vertex and the line segment drawn in Step 1 as a side of an angle, measure a 45-degree angle "going down" from the segment drawn in Step 1. Draw a line segment along that angle that is also about 4.5 units long. Label the open end of that line segment D.
4. Connect points C and D.
5. Open a compass to the distance between A and the place where AB and CD intersect. Place the point at the place where AB and CD intersect and now draw a circle around the two triangles that you made.

Task

Using this Task

Distribute the two-page task to students and read the following or para-phrase it closely.

Who is wearing a T-shirt today? (Identify students who are wearing a T-shirt with a design, picture, or words printed on their shirt.) Does anyone know how this is done? [It is a prepared design that is heat-transferred onto the shirt, or perhaps silk-screened.]

This activity is about someone who has designed a T-shirt logo and needs to describe it to someone over the phone.

Would someone please read the directions? (You may want to ask other students to clarify the directions but do not discuss how to do the task.) Would someone read the aims of the assessment in the box on top of the second activity page?

Since you have to write directions in this problem, you will be communicating mathematically. Think about how well your friend can understand your directions. In fact, when you get done, you can read your directions to yourself as though you were your friend on the other end of the phone. Ask yourself, "Would I know what to draw from the directions?" Think about how accurately Chris would draw the picture from the directions you have given. Will everything in the design be in Chris's picture? Will the design be in the right place on the grid?

Think about how you could check your directions after you are finished. One thing you could do to try checking your work would be to use the blank grid included with the task to try drawing the design from your directions.

Issues for Classroom Use

This task does not require students to use the conventional Cartesian coordinate system. Students may use nonconventional and invented systems as well as conventional coordinate ones for locating the design.

Characterizing Performance

This section offers a characterization of student responses and provides indications of the ways in which the students were successful or unsuccessful in engaging with and completing the task. The descriptions are keyed to the *Core Elements of Performance*. Our global descriptions of student work range from "The student needs significant instruction" to "The student's work meets the essential demands of the task." Samples of student work that exemplify these descriptions of performance are included below, accompanied by commentary on central aspects of each student's response. These sample responses are *representative;* they may not mirror the global description of performance in all respects, being weaker in some and stronger in others.

The characterization of student responses for this task is based on these *Core Elements of Performance:*

1. Locate the placement of all parts of the design (circle, diameter, zigzag) on a grid.
2. Use an efficient and systematic approach (may be an invented system).
3. Give a clear set of directions.

Descriptions of Student Work

The student needs significant instruction.

Student uses no system for locating parts of the design and makes major errors in placement or distorts the shape of the design.

Student A

Student A does not correctly locate any portion of the design. He uses no apparent system for locating the design. His directions allow the triangles to be randomly placed. He seems to make very little attempt to complete the task.

The student needs some instruction.

Student attempts a system for locating all parts of the design but the system does not have the potential for locating points precisely. This results in

Task

errors in placement or a lack of relationship between the whole design and its parts OR considerable effort is needed to follow the directions.

Student B

Student B attempts to locate all parts of the design but has major errors in placement of the shapes because of the system she uses. She gives no size indication for the circle, and her system of describing the rows does not have the potential to allow an accurate representation of the design. The reader needs to make a considerable effort to follow her directions.

The student's work needs to be revised.

Student gives a system that addresses all parts of the design, which has the potential for locating points precisely; but the system is inefficient, resulting in inaccuracies. Some effort may be needed to follow the directions.

Student C

Student C's description is complete in that he addresses all portions of the design. However, his system is somewhat problematic because he refers to the line between the 5 and 6 square and then to the 5 and 6 lines. Since these are not clearly the same, the circle could be distorted. Student C's approach is systematic but not efficient. With some effort the reader is able to follow his reasoning.

The student's work meets the essential demands of the task.

Student gives a complete, efficient system that is capable of locating all parts of the design with reasonable accuracy AND directions are clearly stated and easy to follow.

Student D

Student D correctly locates all of the portions of the design using an efficient coordinate system. Her directions are easy to follow although she has reversed the conventional x and y order, but has not directly communicated that.

Student E

Student E correctly locates all portions of the design using an effective system. His directions are clearly stated and easy to follow, although he has neglected to specify in which order to number the boxes.

① First you get A peice of graph paper.
② You draw a circle in the middle of the paper.
③ Then you make 2 triangles that one is right side up and the other one upside down t the a together.

1. its a 10 by 10 grid, draw that.

2. there is nothing in the top row.

3. The second row has something in it two spaces over from the edge on the right side theres a line near the corner of that square that line continues to make a full circle draw that.

4. Inside the circle there's like a tilted bow start from the middle edge of the circle draw a straght line up from that square up 3 spaces diagnaly. Now, take that line and go down two spaces diagnoly. Now go up diagonaly 3 spaces from that square you should be on the left middle side of the circle. go stright across to reach the middle right side.

First get a pice of 10 by 10 grid paper
then go in the uper left hand corner and
count 5 squares across And the line
thats in between the 5 and 6 square
you are gowing to draw a
cirele starting from the 5 and 6 line
right under it start your circle
your circle should be 10 and a 1/2
centemeters down and 10 and 1/2
cent meters across After you are
done with the circle you need to
look for the center line of the
circle going horizontal Then
draw a line from the left sid. to the
right side going horizontal.
Then go to the left side
of the cewter of the circle and
draw a 5 and 1/2 centemcter
line going diagnol to the right
Then go to the top of your
diagnol line and make 8 and a
1/2 centemeter diagnol line going
down to the right Then after

Student C

you have don that you need to draw
a 5 and $\frac{1}{2}$ centimeter diagnal line
going to the right just to the center.
line of the circle. And you should
have a circle with two triangles
connecting in it It looks like an 8.

The design below, including the 10-by-10 grid, is going to be used on a math team T-shirt. You accidentally took the original design home, and your friend Chris needs it tonight. Chris has no fax machine, but he does have a 10-by-10 grid just like yours (see Chris' grid on the next page). You must call Chris on the telephone and tell him very precisely how to draw the design on his grid.

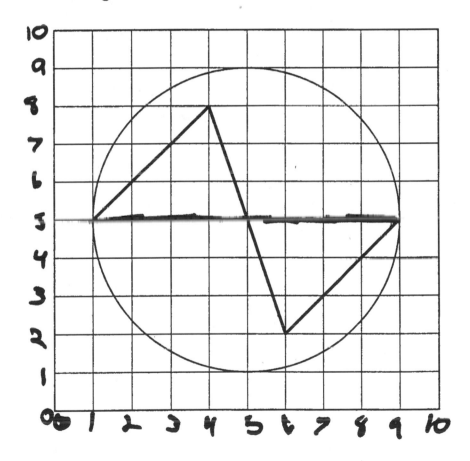

T-shirt Design
Make a 10 X 10 graph. Put a dot on
5,1 , 1,5,5, 9 and 9,5 then connect then to
make a circle, Go to 8,4 and mark
it with a dot. Go to 5,1 and put a dot
connect 8,4 and 5,1 by a straight line.
Put a dot on 5,9 Now draw a straight
line from 5,1 to 5,9 to cut the circle
into two, Put a dot on 2,6 and draw
a straight line from 8,4 to 2,6 Go
to 5,9 and draw a straight line from
5,9 to 2,6

The design below, including the 10-by-10 grid, is going to be used on a math team T-shirt. You accidentally took the original design home, and your friend Chris needs it tonight. Chris has no fax machine, but he does have a 10-by-10 grid just like yours (see Chris' grid on the next page). You must call Chris on the telephone and tell him very precisely how to draw the design on his grid.

1. Make a 10 by 10 grid with the boxes 1/2 on inch wide and 1/2 an inch tall.

2. Number them 1 to 100 starting from the top left-hand corner

3. At the line seperating 42 from 52 make a 4-inch line going from boxes 42 and 52 across to 49 and 59

4. Make a Qaurter of a circle starting at the left edge of the middle line going to the center of 5, 6, 15, and 16.

5. Make another Qaurter of a circle starting at the center of 5, 6, 15, and 16 and ending at the center of 49, 50, 59, and 60.

6. Make another Qaurter of a circle starting at the center of 49, 50, 89, and 60 and ending at the center of 85, 86, 95, and

7. Make another Qaurter of a circle start at the center of 85, 86, 95, and 96 and ending at the center of 41, 42, 51, and 52 which is where you started. You should now have a circle that is 4-inches wide and 4-inches tall. If you have

have a line from the top of the circle
to the bottom of the circle
erase it.
8. Make a line from the center of boxes
14, 15, 24, and 25 to the center of boxes
76, 77, 86, and 87.
9. Now make a line going from the
centers of the boxes 76, 77, 86 and 87.
    end
to the right-hand   of the
line that you made in the beginning.
10. Make a line connecting the
the line that begins at the
    center of 14, 15, 24, 25 to the
    left-hand end of the line
    you made in the beginning.

Select and construct a
graph or other visual
representation for a given
purpose.

Give reason(s) for choice.

Energy

Long Task

Task Description

This task provides a data set of energy use and gross national product for
North and South American countries. It also gives a newspaper article that
claims: "Rich Countries Using Most Energy." Students design a graph or
visual representation of the data that supports the article's claim. They write
a note to the article's author explaining their choice of representation.

Assumed Mathematical Background

It is assumed that students have had experiences in selecting and using
appropriate graphs and other visual representations of data to illustrate
different points of view.

Core Elements of Performance

- select an appropriate graph or visual representation for a given
  purpose
- construct the visual representation completely and accurately
- effectively explain how the selected representation illustrates the
  claim in the article

Circumstances

Grouping:	Following a class introduction, students complete an individual written response.
Materials:	newspapers that illustrate a variety of graphics (for example, *USA Today*), graph paper, compasses, protractors or angle rulers, rulers, and graphing software (optional)
Estimated time:	45 minutes following a 15-minute pre-assessment activity

Energy: Pre-Assessment Study Sheet

As a class

To make sure that you do your best on tomorrow's assessment activity, read the newspaper article, study this data set thoroughly, and read about the terms used in the article.

This is a first draft of an article written by a newspaper reporter.

Rich Countries Using Most Energy

The annual report on wealth and energy was released last week, and as expected, the wealthiest countries in the Western hemisphere are the highest energy users.

The USA and Canada both had per capita GNPs over $15,000 (US$) while the closest runner-up was Venezuela at $3,250 (US$). The same two countries consumed far more energy than the rest of the Americas: Canada and the USA consumed 400 and 350 BTUs per person, respectively. The rest of the countries in the Western hemisphere consumed from 14 to 92 BTUs per person in the last year.

Experts concerned with conservation of natural gas and other natural resources say that the more money people have, the more energy they can afford to purchase. They claim that many wasteful practices are commonplace in the USA and Canada and advocate that an education program be put into place to promote the conservation of natural resources.

The reporter based her article on the following table of data:

Country	Per Capita GNP (US$)	Per Capita Energy Consumption (BTUs)
Argentina	2520	61
Bolivia	570	14
Brazil	2160	47
Canada	16,860	400
Chile	1510	44
Colombia	1240	35
Ecuador	1110	28
Guyana	420	16
Mexico	1770	53
Panama	2130	30
Paraguay	1180	21
Peru	1300	22
Surinam	2450	48
United States	19,870	350
Venezuela	3250	92

1. What do you think "GNP" and "per capita" mean? STOP and THINK. Then read on.

Gross National Product is the amount of money represented in goods and services that are produced in a country in one year. *Per capita* means "per person," so the per capita GNP is the mean or average amount of money produced in the country per person, and it is calculated by dividing the GNP by the number of people living in the country.

2. What do you think "Per Capita Energy Consumption (BTUs)" means? STOP and THINK. Then read on.

BTU is a measure of energy. For example, in stores selling refrigerators and freezers, the average number of BTUs per year needed to operate the appliances is reported so that consumers can understand which products are the most energy-efficient. *Per Capita Energy Consumption* means that all of the energy consumed in the country (as measured in BTUs) is divided by the number of people in the country to find a mean, or an average amount of energy used by each individual in the country.

3. When you read the article, did you understand it thoroughly? Do you now know what GNP is? Do you know what a BTU measures? If these ideas are not clear, ask a question. If there are any other words that you do not understand, look them up in a dictionary.

Energy

> ### This problem gives you the chance to
>
> - *make sense of data as it appears in authentic sources*
> - *select appropriate graphics for a given purpose*
> - *organize and represent data*
> - *communicate your reasons for your selection*

On your own

You are an assistant to a newspaper reporter. The reporter has written the article, "Rich Countries Using Most Energy." You have been assigned to prepare a graphic representation for the article that shows how the wealth of the country *is related* to the energy use in that country. (Use the data in the table to support your graph.)

1. Prepare a careful drawing of your graphic to send to the reporter for consideration. Make sure that the important details are included so that she will not have to call you with any questions.

2. Write a note to the reporter telling her how your graphic supports the article's title.

Task

A Sample Solution

7

Students are asked to produce a graphic that relates wealth to energy use of each individual country. Students need to construct a representation that shows the relationship between two variables simultaneously. A scatter plot on a two-dimensional coordinate graph would be an excellent method. A double bar graph drawn on a doubly scaled vertical axis (for GNP and BTUs) can also effectively show the relationship between the two variables. The critical issue is that the two variables are illustrated simultaneously.

1. See next page.

2. Dear Reporter,
   I chose a scatter plot to represent the relationship between each country's wealth and energy consumption. I put GNP on the horizontal axis to represent the independent variable and BTUs on the vertical axis to represent the dependent variable. The graph shows how different the USA and Canada are compared to the other countries. The graph suggests that the wealthier a country, the more energy it consumes, just as your title claims!

   — A. Student

Relationship between per capita GNP and BTUs of North and South American countries

(Sample scatter plot solution—each dot represents a different nation.)

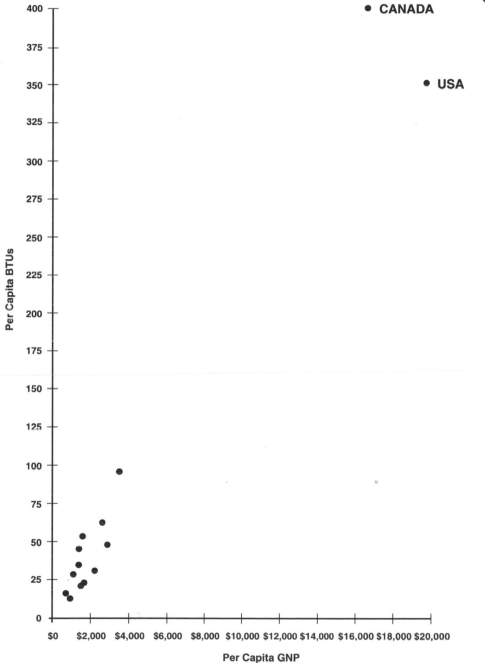

Task

7

Using this Task

Pre-Assessment

The pre-assessment activity will help familiarize students with the context of the task. You may want to do the pre-assessment activity the day *prior* to the assessment. You may wish to arrange that the activity be done in social studies class. The primary purpose of the pre-assessment is to ensure that students understand the meanings of per capita Gross National Product (GNP) and British Thermal Units (BTUs). (The data given in this task reflect per capita income and per capita energy consumption; BTU is a standard unit for measuring energy.) Lack of knowledge of these ideas might hinder performance on the mathematics of the task; all students must have the opportunity to make sense of these concepts.

After you pass out the pre-assessment pages to students, go through the pages as a class and discuss the concepts of per capita GNP and BTUs. Be sure to clarify any misunderstood terms. Students may use these pages and notes from the discussion for the *On your own* section, if they wish.

Assessment

Have special materials available. Pass out the *On your own* page to students. Read the task together. Ask students to tell what is meant by a newspaper "graphic." Illustrate with several examples from a newspaper (for example, *USA Today*). Use the terms "graph" and "visual representation of data" to convey the flexibility of the term "graphic." One of the main purposes of this assessment is to see what methods students select or invent to represent data for a specific purpose.

Review with students the aims of the assessment in the box at the top of page 127 and have them begin working *individually*. Tell the students to work at making an appropriate graphic but to save some time at the end of the class period to answer question 2.

Remind students that they may use their pre-assessment pages to review the meaning of GNP and BTU as they work though the task. If students ask questions, emphasize that it is *their* choice what kind of graphic to do. (Do not suggest any particular graph or visual representation.) You *can* restate that students need to select a graphic that will help the reporter show the *relationship* between energy use of countries and wealth.

Characterizing Performance

This section offers a characterization of student responses and provides indications of the ways in which the students were successful or unsuccessful in engaging with and completing the task. The descriptions are keyed to the *Core Elements of Performance*. Our global descriptions of student work range from "The student needs significant instruction" to "The student's work meets the essential demands of the task." Samples of student work that exemplify these descriptions of performance are included below, accompanied by commentary on central aspects of each student's response. These sample responses are *representative;* they may not mirror the global description of performance in all respects, being weaker in some and stronger in others.

The characterization of student responses for this task is based on these *Core Elements of Performance:*

1. Select an appropriate graph or visual representation for a given purpose.
2. Construct the visual representation completely and accurately.
3. Effectively explain how the selected representation illustrates the claim in the article.

Descriptions of Student Work

The student needs significant instruction.

Student selects a graphic that does not effectively relate the two variables (per capita GNP and BTUs) simultaneously and the graphic has inaccuracies or lacks clarity. Student may or may not have written a note to the reporter.

Student A

Student A selects a bar graph representation that contains major inaccuracies: the student rank orders the countries according to income and records their per capita GNPs along the *x*-axis with no attention to scale. Furthermore, the student's graph seems to relate the rank ordering of per capita incomes to the "magnitude" of the countries from their position along the *y*-axis (which has no meaning).

Task

7

Student B

Student B selects a pictographic representation that tries to show the relationship of the countries with regard to one variable. It is unclear which variable relates to the height of the "ships." The student does not complete the graph, nor provide complete labels. This graphic has the potential for representing the relationship between per capita GNP and BTU for the given countries. For example, the size of the rocket could indicate relative wealth and the height of the rocket could indicate energy consumption. A successful pictograph of this type would require the student to use a great deal of proportional and visual reasoning.

The student needs some instruction.

Student selects a graphic representation that does not effectively relate the two variables (per capita GNP and BTUs) simultaneously; however, the graphic selected is clearly drawn and accurate (that is, containing complete and appropriate labels, title, scale), OR student selects a representation that has the potential for relating the two variables simultaneously but has major inaccuracies (for example, mistakes in scale). Student may or may not have written an explanation to the reporter.

Student C

Student C constructs two independent bar graphs, one for each variable (per capita GNP and BTU), which do not show a relationship between the two variables. The student uses appropriate scaling and clearly draws the graphic, but does not clearly label and title the graphs. The note does not relate the graphs to the reporter's purpose.

Student D

Student D attempts to relate the two variables with a scatter plot. However, the graph contains major inaccuracies: the student switches scales on both axes. Further, the student plots points that do not represent the given data (for example, there is a point at 2 BTUs and $3000, and no country meets that description). The student also shows confusion about the continuous nature of the *x*- and *y*-axes; all points are plotted at *y* values.

The student's work needs to be revised.

Student selects a representation that simultaneously relates the two variables (per capita GNP and BTUs) but the graphic may have some *minor* inaccuracies or lack clarity. The explanation of the selection may be missing or fail to address the purpose of the article.

Student E

Student E's representation simultaneously relates the two variables but not in a completely successful way. Placing two bar graphs on two different axes makes it difficult to see a relationship. The graph is completely and accurately labeled and the student uses a scale completely and correctly for the GNP, but incorrectly for the BTUs.

Student F

Student F uses a scatter-plot representation that effectively relates the two variables and constructs it completely and accurately. The student neglects to write a note to the newspaper reporter.

The student's work meets the essential demands of the task.

Student selects a representation that simultaneously relates the two variables (per capita GNP and BTUs) and constructs the graphic with accuracy and clarity (complete and appropriate labels, title, scale), AND the student's explanation addresses the purpose of the article.

Student G

Student G uses a double bar graph successfully to illustrate a relationship between the two variables, and he includes appropriate scales, labels, and titles. His note to the reporter addresses how the graphic relates to the article's purpose.

Student A

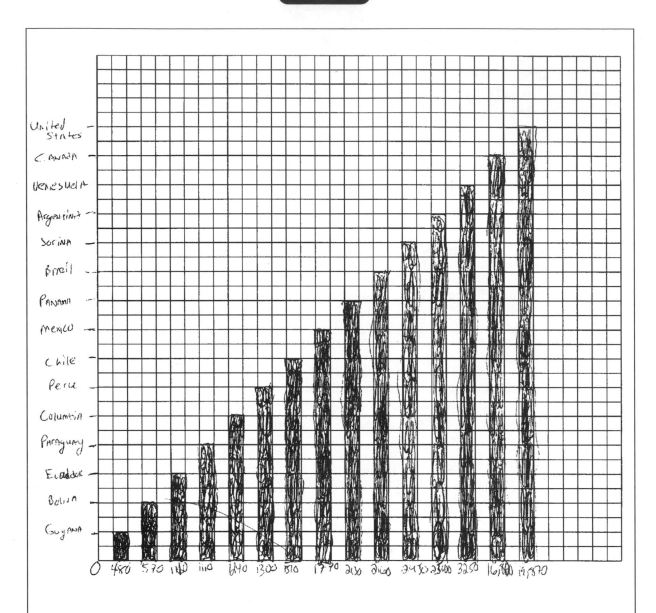

Student B

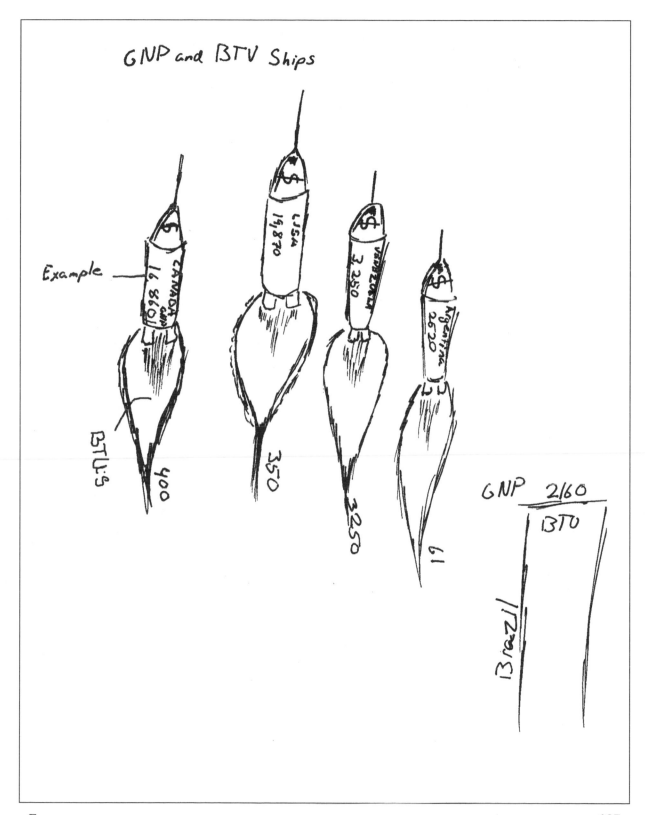

GNP and BTV Ships

Example

BTU's

CANADA
GNP 16,980

400

USA
19,870

350

VENEZUELA
3,250

3250

Argentina
2,620

19

GNP 2160
BTU

Brazil

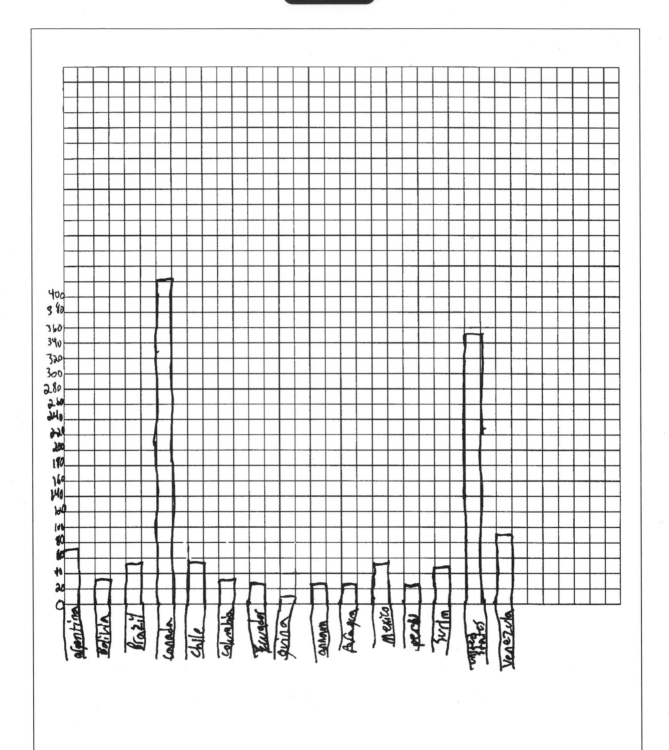

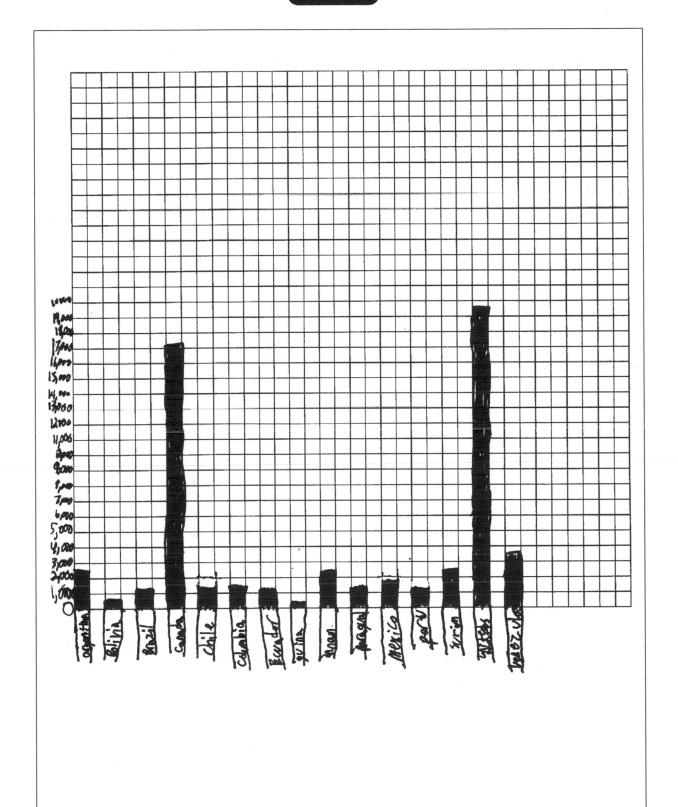

Student C

The bars show more better on how to see which has more money.

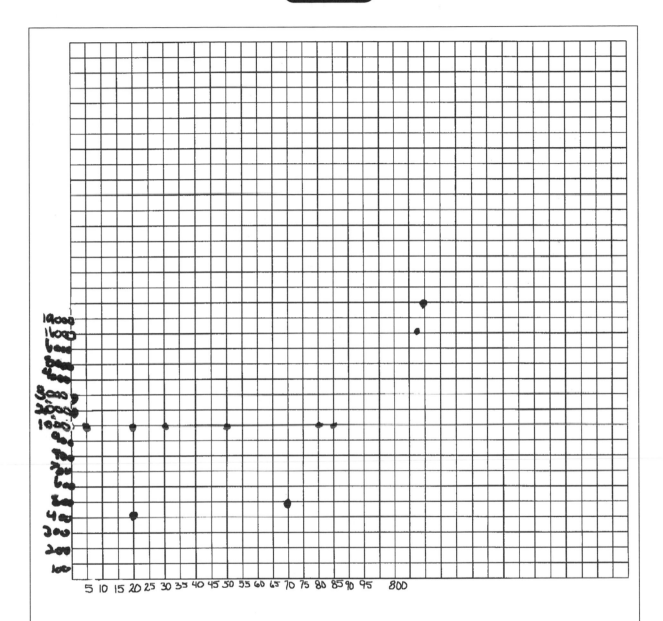

Note: This graphic is very simple to figure
out you simpley conect the dots to
least to greatest and that is called
a conner graph. That is the graphic
~~that~~ I made

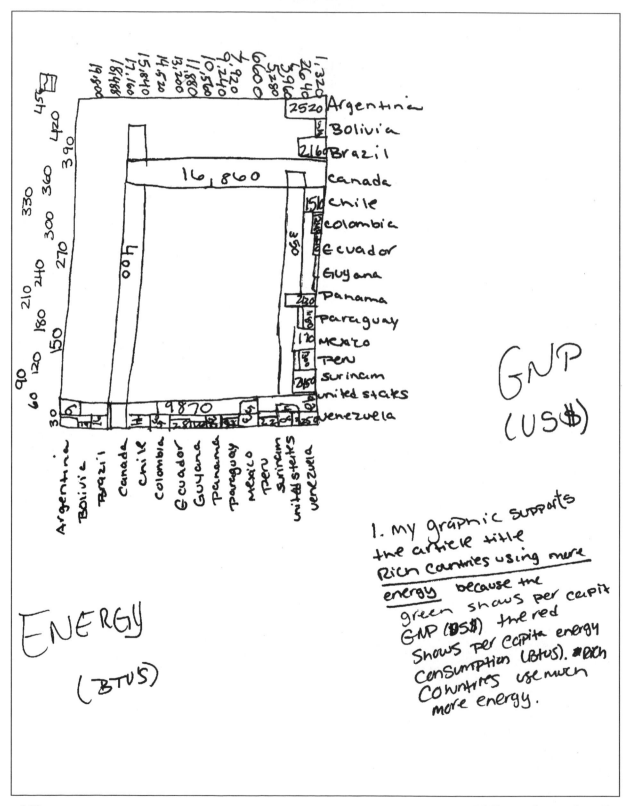

ENERGY

(BTUS)

GNP

(US$)

1. My graphic supports the article title Rich countries using more energy because the green shows per capita GNP (US$) the red shows per capita energy consumption (BTUS). #Rich countries use much more energy.

Student F

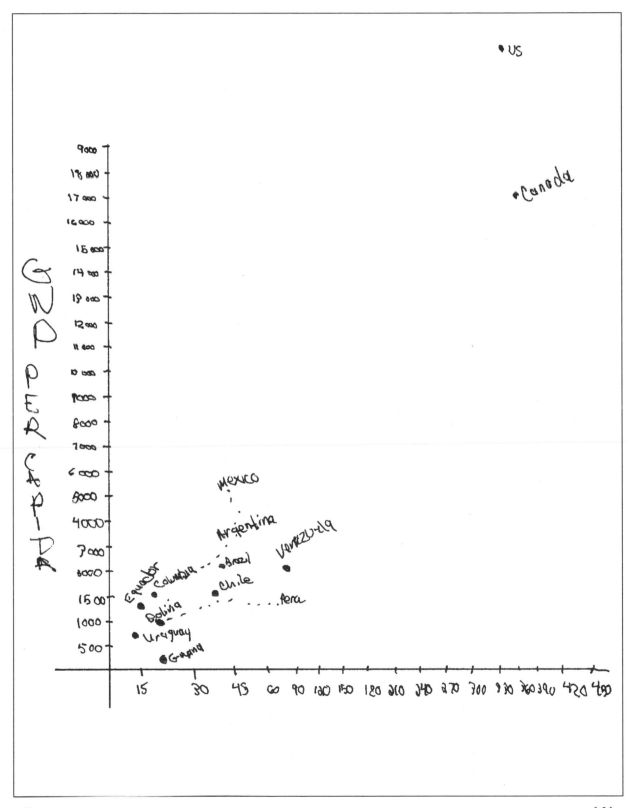

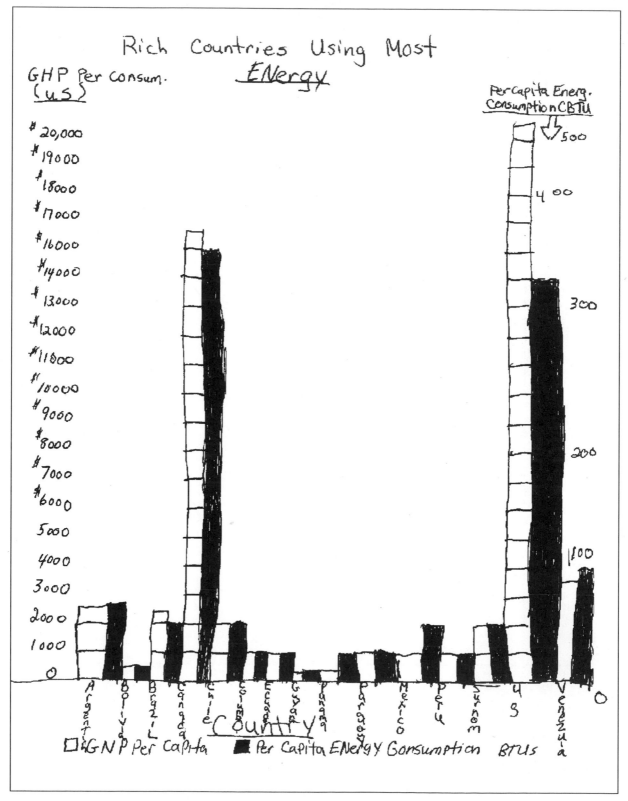

Rich Countries Using Most ENergy

GHP Per Consum. (us)

Per Capita Energ. Consumption CBTU

□ GNP Per Capita   ■ Per Capita ENergy Consumption BTUs

Dear Author,

I think that my graphic best supports your title because it shows the Country's GNP Per Capita and It's energy Consumption Side by Side, therefore you Can visually compare the GNP and Energy Consumption. You Can also see that the higher the GNP the Higher the Energy consumption.

Sincerely,

Best Guess?

Overview

**Choose appropriate
statistical tools to
analyze data.**

**Draw conclusions based
on statistical measures.**

Short Task

Task Description

Students are given data sets on three people's estimates of when 30 seconds has passed. Students use the data sets to decide who is best at estimating a 30-second interval.

Assumed Mathematical Background

It is assumed that students have had experience with using statistical tools (including measures of center and spread) to analyze data.

Core Elements of Performance

- choose appropriate statistical tools to analyze variation and center

- apply statistical tools accurately

- use results from data analysis to draw and support conclusions for a situation

Circumstances

Grouping:	Students complete an individual written response.
Materials:	No special materials are needed for this task.
Estimated time:	15 minutes

Best Guess?

This problem gives you the chance to

- *choose appropriate statistical tools*
- *apply statistical tools accurately*
- *analyze data and use results to draw and support conclusions*

On your own

Hugh, Rita, and Sandy were trying to see who could make the closest estimate of when a 30-second interval had passed. They took turns guessing while someone else kept time with a stopwatch.

When it was Hugh's turn to guess, the following times were recorded from the stopwatch:

31   25   32   27   28

When it was Rita's turn to guess, the following times were recorded from the stopwatch:

37   19   40   36   22

When it was Sandy's turn to guess, the following times were recorded from the stopwatch:

32   38   24   32   32

1. Who do you think is best at estimating 30 seconds? _____
2. Give reasons for your choice.

A Sample Solution

Hugh is the best guesser because the range of his guesses is smallest (the difference between his lowest guess and his highest guess is only 7 seconds), and he is never more than 5 seconds off on any turn. Hugh's median guess is 28, only 2 seconds off. Sandy's median guess is 32 which is also only 2 seconds off, but she has two guesses that are 6 and 8 seconds off and on opposite sides of the 30-second mark, making her range of guesses larger than Hugh's. In this situation, the mean is not a reasonable measure to evaluate the people's guessing ability because Rita's guesses are between 6 and 11 seconds off and yet balance out with the mean to be very close (30.8) to the desired goal of 30 seconds.

More on the Mathematics

Students may choose to use a number of different statistical measures in determining their answer. For this task, spread of the data around 30 is the most powerful measure for determining who is the best guesser. A strong argument would consider measures of center and the spread of the data and support a choice based on these measures and their relationship. Using these tools, Hugh and/or Sandy could be supported as being the better guesser. Any combination of statistical measures could not support Rita as a reasonable choice.

The spread of the data shows that Hugh does the best with his guessing. Rita's guesses are very spread out (range of 19 to 40, spread of 21). Sandy's guesses are more spread out (range of 24 to 38, spread of 14) than Hugh's, whose data is the most compact (range of 25 to 32, spread of 7).

Sandy has a mode guess of 32, neither of the other two has a mode guess. The mode itself is not a very useful statistic for this situation. What makes Sandy's mode worth noting is that she is very close to the desired goal of 30 seconds. To argue that she is the better guesser *only* because she guessed the same number three times is a weak response.

Looking at median, Hugh and Sandy would be tied as the better guesser with a median guess of 28 and 32, respectively, (both 2 from 30) compared to Rita's median of 36.

Regarding mean, Rita has a mean guess of 30.8, Sandy has a mean guess of 31.6, and Hugh has a mean guess of 28.6. The back-and-forth guessing by Rita makes this a weak measure in helping to decide who is the better guesser.

Task

Using this Task

Review the aims of the assessment in the box at the top of the activity page. Read the problem aloud to your students. Because this task is short and straightforward, it would be appropriate simply to hand out the task and direct students to read and answer the questions individually.

Issues for Classroom Use

At first glance, this problem appears small and contained when actually it provides an opportunity to see which statistical tools students bring to bear on a problem as well as how they make sense of these measures. The fact that some students use only the mean to justify their choice, failing to think about the range and what it says about the data set, shows a lack of understanding of statistics on the part of the student. Students must also consider the spreads of the data for each guesser in order to address the task completely.

Characterizing Performance

This section offers a characterization of student responses and provides indications of the ways in which the students were successful or unsuccessful in engaging with and completing the task. The descriptions are keyed to the *Core Elements of Performance*. Our global descriptions of student work range from "The student needs significant instruction" to "The student's work meets the essential demands of the task." Samples of student work that exemplify these descriptions of performance are included below, accompanied by commentary on central aspects of each student's response. These sample responses are *representative;* they may not mirror the global description of performance in all respects, being weaker in some and stronger in others.

The characterization of student responses for this task is based on these *Core Elements of Performance:*

1. Choose appropriate statistical tools to analyze variation and center.
2. Apply statistical tools accurately.
3. Use results from data analysis to draw and support conclusions for a situation.

Descriptions of Student Work

The student's work cannot be assessed.

Student A

Student A has posed an answer with a reason that does not make sense, and there is no evidence of data analysis. This work is unscorable.

The student needs significant instruction.

Student selects and attempts to apply inappropriate or vague/unclear statistical tool(s) (for example, student might find the sum for each set of data).

Student B

Student B found the sums of the data points, which alone is not helpful for deciding the best guesser. Further, while the reasons given refer to Hugh's having the "most closest guess to 30 seconds," there is no method or tool used to provide the data analysis needed to support this reason.

Task

The student needs some instruction.

Student selects (or invents) and applies statistical tools that provide information about either the variation/spread or the center OR tools and calculations are absent or unclear. There is, however, evidence in the reasoning that the student was considering a method that would take into account both measure of variation and center.

Student C

Student C finds the mean for each data set. While the student refers to the notion of variation/spread ("Hugh got close to 30 every time"), there is no defined statistical method or tool that is applied to the other data sets. The student needs some instruction and not just a revision of his work.

Student D

Student D is not clear about the method of data analysis. The reference to Sandy as the best guesser, "Because she was the closest to 30 almost She got 32 seconds 3 times and than she was of(f) a little bit on the other two," seems to indicate that she is making a count of how often the guessers are "close" to 30, using the mode of the data set. While Student D seems to understand that the variation/spread is an important feature in solving the problem and also attends to a measure of center, the statistical tool being used is vague and hasn't been applied systematically across data sets.

The student's work needs to be revised.

Student selects and applies statistical tools that provide information about both the spread and the center (for example, student attempts to count the number of times the guess is within 2 seconds of 30; student attempts to use both the median and the range of guesses). While the student recognizes the importance of both types of information, there is no evidence that the student realizes that for this context the variation is the more important of the two aspects. There may be some calculation errors or problems in articulating reasoning.

No student examples at this level.

The student's work meets the essential demands of the task.

Student correctly calculates or states measures that address both the spread and the center for two or three sets of data, recognizes the greater importance of the measure of spread for this context, and in the justification for the best guesser compares the statistics found between at least two of the guessers.

Student E

Student E found the average (mean) for each individual and also applied a statistic of variation: count the number of times the guess is within 5 seconds of 30. Student E points out that all of Hugh's guesses were within 5 seconds and that all of Rita's guesses were outside the 5-second range. The reasons for Student E's choice clearly indicate the importance of both center and spread for this context, and that the measure of spread is the more important factor in making a decision.

This problem gives you the chance to

■ *choose appropriate statistical tools*

■ *apply statistical tools accurately*

■ *analyze data and use results to draw and support conclusions*

On your own

Hugh, Rita, and Sandy were trying to see who could make the closest estimate of when a 30-second interval had passed. They took turns guessing while someone else kept time with a stopwatch.

When it was Hugh's turn to guess, the following times were recorded from the stopwatch:

31	25	32	27	28

When it was Rita's turn to guess, the following times were recorded from the stopwatch:

37	19	40	36	22

When it was Sandy's turn to guess, the following times were recorded from the stopwatch:

32	38	24	32	32

1. Who do you think is best at estimating 30 seconds? *Hugh*
2. Give reasons for your choice.

I saw that he had more guesses.

This problem gives you the chance to

- *choose appropriate statistical tools*
- *apply statistical tools accurately*
- *analyze data and use results to draw and support conclusions*

On your own

Hugh, Rita, and Sandy were trying to see who could make the closest estimate of when a 30-second interval had passed. They took turns guessing while someone else kept time with a stopwatch.

When it was Hugh's turn to guess, the following times were recorded from the stopwatch:

31   25   32   27   28   143 total sec

When it was Rita's turn to guess, the following times were recorded from the stopwatch:

37   19   40   36   22   154 total sec

When it was Sandy's turn to guess, the following times were recorded from the stopwatch:

32   38   24   32   32   158 total sec

1. Who do you think is best at estimating 30 seconds? _____ Hugh

2. Give reasons for your choice. Hugh be is because he had the most closest guess to 30 seconds and because he had the lowest number of seconds, when you add them up.

This problem gives you the chance to

- *choose appropriate statistical tools*
- *apply statistical tools accurately*
- *analyze data and use results to draw and support conclusions*

On your own

Hugh, Rita, and Sandy were trying to see who could make the closest estimate of when a 30-second interval had passed. They took turns guessing while someone else kept time with a stopwatch.

When it was Hugh's turn to guess, the following times were recorded from the stopwatch:

31   25   32   27   28   *28.6*

When it was Rita's turn to guess, the following times were recorded from the stopwatch:

37   19   40   36   22   *30.8*

When it was Sandy's turn to guess, the following times were recorded from the stopwatch:

32   38   24   32   32   *31.6*

1. Who do you think is best at estimating 30 seconds? *Hugh* and *Rita*
2. Give reasons for your choice. *Hugh got close to 30 every time*
Hugh averaged 28.6
Rita Averaged 30.8 Add the 5#'s togather and ÷ by 5

This problem gives you the chance to

- *choose appropriate statistical tools*
- *apply statistical tools accurately*
- *analyze data and use results to draw and support conclusions*

On your own

Hugh, Rita, and Sandy were trying to see who could make the closest estimate of when a 30-second interval had passed. They took turns guessing while someone else kept time with a stopwatch.

When it was Hugh's turn to guess, the following times were recorded from the stopwatch:

       31   25   32   27   28

When it was Rita's turn to guess, the following times were recorded from the stopwatch:

       37   19   40   36   22

When it was Sandy's turn to guess, the following times were recorded from the stopwatch:

       32   38   24   32   32

1. Who do you think is best at estimating 30 seconds

Sandy

2. Give reasons for your choice.

Because she was the Closest to 30 about she got 32 seconds 3 times and than she was of little bit on the other two

Student E

This problem gives you the chance to

- *choose appropriate statistical tools*
- *apply statistical tools accurately*
- *analyze data and use results to draw and support conclusions*

On your own

Hugh, Rita, and Sandy were trying to see who could make the closest estimate of when a 30-second interval had passed. They took turns guessing while someone else kept time with a stopwatch.

When it was Hugh's turn to guess, the following times were recorded from the stopwatch:

31   25   32   27   28   *Average: 28.6*

When it was Rita's turn to guess, the following times were recorded from the stopwatch:

37   19   40   36   22   *Average: 30.8*

When it was Sandy's turn to guess, the following times were recorded from the stopwatch:

32   38   24   32   32   *Average: 31.6*

1. Who do you think is best at estimating 30 seconds? __*Hugh*__

2. Give reasons for your choice.

   I think that Hugh was the best because he always guessed at least 5 seconds within the 30 second range. Also even though Rita had a better average she was always far from 30 sec.

Fractions of a Square

Use numerical and spatial sense to identify and compare fractional parts.

Use numerical and spatial sense to divide a square into several different-sized fractions.

Short Task

Task Description

Students are given a square divided into several pieces. They must determine what fractional part each piece represents. Students estimate which piece(s) are close to given fractions. Lastly, they are asked to design their own fraction square under specified constraints.

Assumed Mathematical Background

It is assumed that students have a background in rational numbers.

Core Elements of Performance

- correctly identify fractional parts of a whole
- justify names for fractional parts using spatial and numerical reasoning and coherent arguments
- reason about sizes of rational numbers
- design own "fractions of a square" within constraints

Circumstances

Grouping:	Students complete an individual written response.
Materials:	No special materials are needed for this task.
Estimated time:	25 minutes

Fractions of a Square

This problem gives you the chance to

- *analyze and reason about rational numbers*
- *use spatial and numerical reasoning*

On your own

The large outer square represents 1 whole unit. It has been partitioned into pieces. Each piece is identified with a letter.

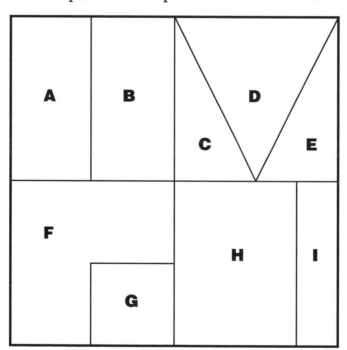

1. Decide what fraction each piece is in relation to the whole square, and write that fraction on the shape.

2. Explain how you know the fractional name for each of the following pieces.

A

C

D

F

3. Identify a piece or collection of pieces from the square that will give you an amount close to:

a. $\frac{1}{5}$

b. $\frac{2}{3}$

4. a. Design your own fraction square using the square below. Your square must contain at least four different-sized fractional pieces other than $\frac{1}{2}$. At least two of your fractional pieces have to be a size different from what is in the original square (used for problems 1, 2, and 3).

b. Give the fractional names for each of your pieces.

A Sample Solution

1. A = $\frac{1}{8}$ B = $\frac{1}{8}$ C = $\frac{1}{16}$

   D = $\frac{1}{8}$ E = $\frac{1}{16}$ F = $\frac{3}{16}$

   G = $\frac{1}{16}$ H = $\frac{3}{16}$ I = $\frac{1}{16}$

2. A: The square is divided into four equal parts, so each part is $\frac{1}{4}$ of the square. The part with A in it is divided into two equal parts and half of a fourth is an eighth, so A must be $\frac{1}{8}$.

C: If you cut D in half you would have two Cs. E is the same size as C. C, D, and E make up $\frac{1}{4}$ of the square. If four Cs fit in $\frac{1}{4}$ of the square, then four would fit in each of the other three fourths. Thus, 16 Cs would make the whole square. So C is $\frac{1}{16}$.

D: C is half of D and C is $\frac{1}{16}$. Since D is equal to two Cs, D must be $\frac{2}{16}$. You can rename $\frac{2}{16}$ as $\frac{1}{8}$.

F: The part of the square with F and G is $\frac{1}{4}$ of the whole square. If you take this part and divide it up into four equal pieces (the size of G), then you would see that F would be represented by three of these pieces. Each of these G-sized pieces is $\frac{1}{16}$ of the whole square, so F must be $\frac{3}{16}$.

Task 9

3a. Close to $\frac{1}{5}$—Any combination of the fractional pieces that equals $\frac{1}{4}$ is close to $\frac{1}{5}$, such as A *and* B; C, D, *and* E; F *and* G; and finally, H *and* I. However, combinations and pieces that add up to $\frac{3}{16}$ are actually *closer* to $\frac{1}{5}$; examples are piece F, or piece H, or a combination of pieces C, E, *and* I.

3b. Close to $\frac{2}{3}$—Any combination of the fractional pieces that equals $\frac{5}{8}$ is close to $\frac{2}{3}$; possible answers are A, B, D, F, *and* G; F, G, H, I, *and* A. However, combinations that add up to $\frac{11}{16}$ are actually *closer* to $\frac{2}{3}$. Some combinations are: A, B, C, D, E, *and* F; F, G, H, I, D, *and* C, etc.

4. Any "fraction square" with at least four different-sized pieces other than $\frac{1}{2}$ and at least two pieces other than $\frac{1}{8}$, $\frac{1}{16}$, and $\frac{3}{16}$.
Two possible responses:

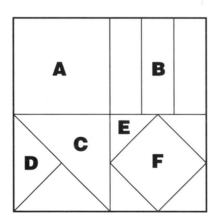

$A = \frac{1}{4}$ $B = \frac{1}{12}$

$C = \frac{1}{8}$ $D = \frac{1}{16}$

$E = \frac{1}{32}$ $F = \frac{4}{32} = \frac{1}{8}$

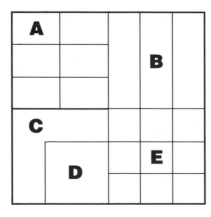

$A = \frac{1}{24}$ $B = \frac{1}{12}$

$C = \frac{5}{36}$ $D = \frac{4}{36} = \frac{1}{9}$

$E = \frac{1}{36}$

Using this Task

Review with students the aims of the assessment given in the box at the top of the activity page. Read through the task with your students.

Point out to students that they are to:

- Decide what fractional part each piece represents given that the original square represents *one whole unit*.

- Record these solutions and give reasons for how they determined the pieces asked about in question 2.

- Determine which piece(s) are close to the given fractions in question 3.

- Design their own fraction squares that meet the given conditions.

Issues for Classroom Use

Students may approach this task using different forms of reasoning. Some use a visual/analytic while others use estimation. There may be some students who use visual analysis on some pieces and estimation on others. Both are valid and have the potential for yielding accurate responses.

Question 3 asks students to determine which fractional pieces are close to given fractions. A more challenging question would ask students which fractional pieces are *closest* to the given fractions. This question may be used as an extension of the activity.

Task

Characterizing Performance

This section offers a characterization of student responses and provides indications of the ways in which the students were successful or unsuccessful in engaging with and completing the task. The descriptions are keyed to the *Core Elements of Performance.* Our global descriptions of student work range from "The student needs significant instruction" to "The student's work meets the essential demands of the task." Samples of student work that exemplify these descriptions of performance are included below, accompanied by commentary on central aspects of each student's response. These sample responses are *representative;* they may not mirror the global description of performance in all respects, being weaker in some and stronger in others.

The characterization of student responses for this task is based on these *Core Elements of Performance:*

1. Correctly identify fractional parts of a whole.
2. Justify names for fractional parts using spatial and numerical reasoning and coherent arguments.
3. Reason about sizes of rational numbers.
4. Design own "fractions of a square" within constraints.

Descriptions of Student Work

The student needs significant instruction.

Student may label some fractional pieces correctly, but shows little evidence or serious errors in either knowledge of fractions or in reasoning about fractions.

Student A

Student A regards each fourth of the square as "one whole," but is inconsistent within this framework. Student A gives a reason for naming only one piece in the square in question 2. Since he does not answer question 4, there is little evidence of his understanding beyond $\frac{1}{2}$ (which most primary grade students know).

The student needs some instruction.

Student successfully labels most fractional pieces but reasoning is weak or incomplete.

Student B

Throughout Student B's responses, the quarter square is interpreted as the unit instead of the entire square. Partial understanding is demonstrated: the total of the fractional pieces of a unit must equal 1; a fraction square in question 4 is appropriately drawn and each piece labeled correctly. (Note: Even though C, D, and E in question 1 are misnamed, together they make one whole.) Student B's knowledge and reasoning about fractions is incomplete.

The student's work needs to be revised.

Student correctly labels most of the fractional pieces (one or two errors are okay) and demonstrates at least partially correct visual and numerical reasoning about fractions.

Student C

Student C correctly identifies all the pieces of the fraction square in question 1 and shows good reasoning in question 2 for the three parts answered. However, the evidence of reasoning is only partial since the answers to question 3 are incorrect, and in question 4 the student has attended to only one constraint (differently-sized fractions) and has neglected to use fractions that have a sum of exactly 1.

The student's work meets the essential demands of the task.

Student demonstrates strong reasoning about fractions and the relationships among them.

Student D

Student D demonstrates strong reasoning and understanding of fractions. While he answers question 3b incorrectly, he offers a clear explanation of his reasoning. This allows us to speculate that he was thinking of $\frac{1}{3}$. In question 4, Student D calls several fractional pieces by the same name— $\frac{1}{64}$. Even though they are drawn as slightly different sizes, it is clear that they are intended to be equal parts.

This problem gives you the chance to

■ *analyze and reason about rational numbers*

■ *use spatial and numerical reasoning*

On your own

The large outer square represents 1 whole unit. It has been partitioned into pieces. Each piece is identified with a letter.

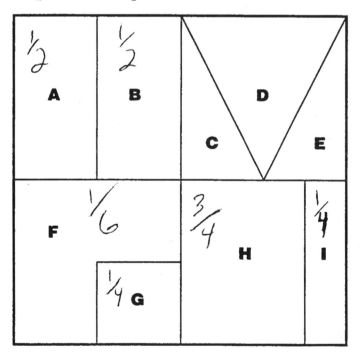

1. Decide what fraction each piece is in relation to the whole square, and write that fraction on the shape.

2 Explain how you know the fractional name for each of the
 following pieces.

 A A is ½ because the sq. is cut in two so that
    makes B ½.

 C

 D

 F F is ⅙

3. Identify a piece or collection of pieces from the square that
   will give you an amount close to:

 a. $\frac{1}{5}$ F, G, H, I

 b. $\frac{2}{3}$

4. a. Design your own fraction square using the square below. Your square must contain at least 4 differently sized fractional pieces, other than $\frac{1}{2}$. At least two of your fractional pieces have to be a size different from what is in the original square (used for problems 1, 2, and 3).

   b. Give the fractional names for each of your pieces.

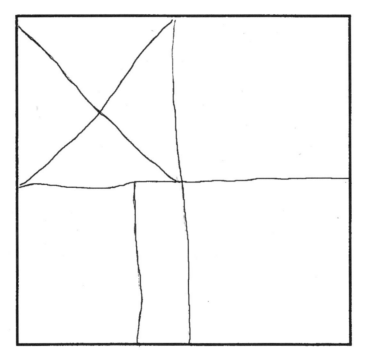

Student B

This problem gives you the chance to

■ *analyze and reason about rational numbers*

■ *use spatial and numerical reasoning*

On your own

The large outer square represents 1 whole unit. It has been partitioned into pieces. Each piece is identified with a letter.

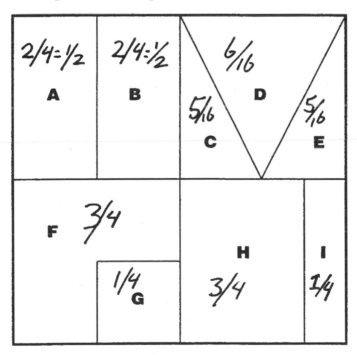

1. Decide what fraction each piece is in relation to the whole square, and write that fraction on the shape.

2 Explain how you know the fractional name for each of the following pieces.

A I decided by useing F and G making G Part of it a 4th and then useing Pices.

C By Dividing half wich eqaled C and E so then I put it into 16 the and I new that D = C and e together.

D I used C and E to help me.

F By Divieding into 4ths and 6 eqaled ¼ E & F had the Rest.

3. Identify a piece or collection of pieces from the square that will give you an amount close to:

a. $\frac{1}{5}$ A or F

b. $\frac{2}{3}$ D

Student B

4. a. Design your own fraction square using the square below.
Your square must contain at least 4 differently sized fractional pieces, other than $\frac{1}{2}$. At least two of your fractional pieces have to be a size different from what is in the
original square (used for problems 1, 2, and 3).

b. Give the fractional names for each of your pieces.

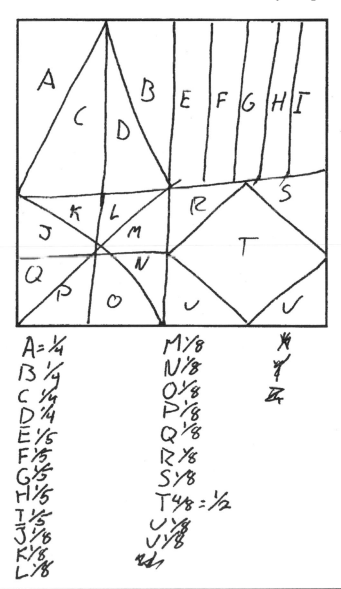

A = ¼
B ¼
C ¼
D ¼
E ⅕
F ⅕
G ⅕
H ⅕
I ⅕
J ⅛
K ⅛
L ⅛

M ⅛
N ⅛
O ⅛
P ⅛
Q ⅛
R ⅛
S ⅛
T ⁴⁄₈ = ½
U ⅛
V ⅛

> ### This problem gives you the chance to
>
> ■ *analyze and reason about rational numbers*
>
> ■ *use spatial and numerical reasoning*

On your own

The large outer square represents 1 whole unit. It has been partitioned into pieces. Each piece is identified with a letter.

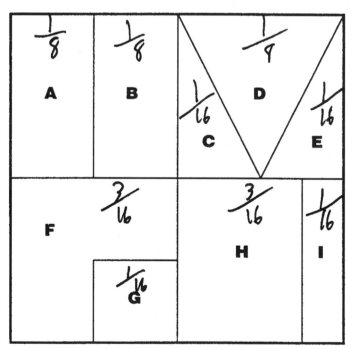

1. Decide what fraction each piece is in relation to the whole square, and write that fraction on the shape.

2 Explain how you know the fractional name for each of the
following pieces.

A I imagined the square being cut into
fourths, then spliting the fourths in half,
then count them up and got 8 and 1 of those 8.

C I imagined the square infourths, then
spliting the fourths into triangles like C and
counted them up and got 16 and 1 of those 16.

D I imagined the square in fourths, then split
the fourths into triangles and got 16
then I counted the number of triangles that covered
F D and got 2.

3. Identify a piece or collection of pieces from the square that
will give you an amount close to:

a. $\frac{1}{5}$ A, B, C, D, E, G, I.

b. $\frac{2}{3}$ J, H,

4. a. Design your own fraction square using the square below. Your square must contain at least 4 differently sized fractional pieces, other than $\frac{1}{2}$. At least two of your fractional pieces have to be a size different from what is in the original square (used for problems 1, 2, and 3).

b. Give the fractional names for each of your pieces.

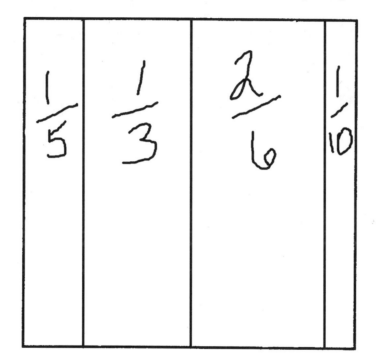

This problem gives you the chance to

■ *analyze and reason about rational numbers*

■ *use spatial and numerical reasoning*

On your own

The large outer square represents 1 whole unit. It has been partitioned into pieces. Each piece is identified with a letter.

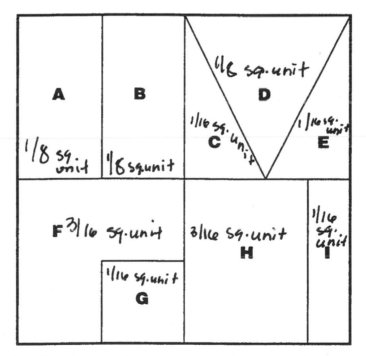

1. Decide what fraction each piece is in relation to the whole square, and write that fraction on the shape.

2 Explain how you know the fractional name for each of the
following pieces.

A A+E together = ¼ sq. Unit and A is half of
~~that~~ One fourth so it is ⅛ sq. Unit.

C If I made a rectangle using C+E I would
get ⅛ and C is half of That ⅛ making
it 1/16

D After C+E making ⅛ there is ⅛ left in
the ¼ square so D is ⅛

F Piece 6 was as wide a half of the ¼
Section but it only went up halfway in that
Section so it couldn't be ⅛ it was 1/16
So F took the remaining 3/16

3. Identify a piece or collection of pieces from the square that
will give you an amount close to:

a. $\frac{1}{5}$ 3/16 would be closest to 1/5
   piece   H or F

b. $\frac{2}{3}$ Pieces A, B, and D would equal 3/8
   which is close to 2/3

Student D

4. a. Design your own fraction square using the square below. Your square must contain at least 4 differently sized fractional pieces, other than $\frac{1}{2}$. At least two of your fractional pieces have to be a size different from what is in the original square (used for problems 1, 2, and 3).

b. Give the fractional names for each of your pieces.

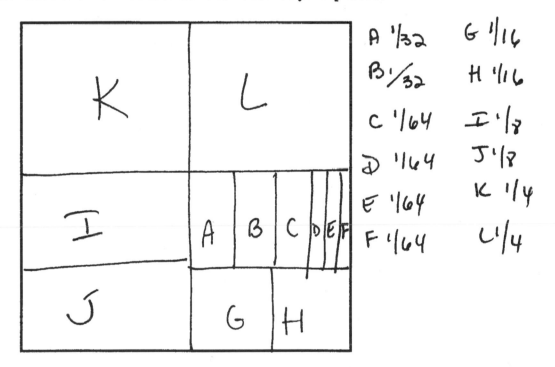

A $\frac{1}{32}$ G $\frac{1}{16}$

B $\frac{1}{32}$ H $\frac{1}{16}$

C $\frac{1}{64}$ I $\frac{1}{8}$

D $\frac{1}{64}$ J $\frac{1}{8}$

E $\frac{1}{64}$ K $\frac{1}{4}$

F $\frac{1}{64}$ L $\frac{1}{4}$

Identify and justify
similar triangles.

Generalize 1- and 2-
dimensional growth
using variables.

Similar Triangles

Short Task

Task Description

This task is a collection of related questions on similar triangles and their
relationships. Students are asked to identify which triangles are similar to a
given one and give reasons for their choice. They are then asked to give the
height, base length, and area for similar triangles of given scale factors for
specific and general cases.

Assumed Mathematical Background

It is assumed that students have had experiences with similar figures and
scale factor.

Core Elements of Performance

- identify and define similar triangles
- use scale factor of similar triangles to determine linear and area
  measures
- use variables to represent 1- and 2-dimensional growth in similar
  triangles

Circumstances

Grouping:	Students complete an individual written response.
Materials:	grid paper, rulers, and protractors or angle rulers
Estimated time:	10 minutes

Similar Triangles

This problem gives you the chance to
- *reason about similar figures and scale factor*
- *generalize using variables*

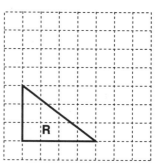

On your own

1. Which of the triangles below is similar to Triangle R?

Triangle 1

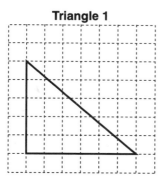

Triangle 2

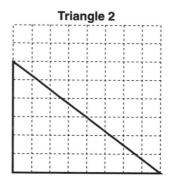

Triangle 3

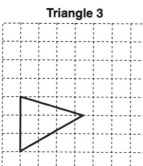

Triangle 4

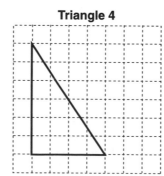

2. Describe how you decided which triangle was similar to R.

_____

_____

_____

_____

3. If Triangle R is enlarged, what will height and base lengths be for the new triangle for the following scale factors?

	Height	**Base**
scale factor of 2.5	_____	_____
scale factor of 10	_____	_____
scale factor of n	_____	_____

4. If Triangle R is enlarged, what will the area be for the new triangle for the following scale factors?

scale factor of 2.5   _____

scale factor of 10   _____

scale factor of n _____

Task **A Sample Solution**

10

1. Triangle 2 is similar to Triangle R.

2. The sides of Triangle 2 are twice as long as the corresponding sides of the original triangle.

   OR

   Corresponding angles for the two triangles are the same size.

   OR

   Triangles 1, 3, and 4 are not similar to Triangle R because the corresponding angles are not the same size and the corresponding sides are not proportional.

3.

Scale Factor	Height	Base
2.5	7.5	10
10	30	40
n	$3n$	$4n$

4.

Scale Factor	Area
2.5	37.5 units^2
10	600 units^2
n	$6n^2$ units^2

More about the Mathematics

Students often assume incorrectly that if the scale factor for similar triangles is "n," then the relation between the lengths of the sides of the two figures and the relation between the areas of the figures are the same—that both are n. In fact, the lengths of the sides grow by a factor of n while the area grows by a factor of n^2.

Using this Task

Review the aims of the assessment in the box at the top of the activity page. Read the problem aloud to your students. Because this task is short and straightforward, it would be appropriate simply to hand out the task and direct students to read and answer the questions individually.

Characterizing Performance

Task

This section offers a characterization of student responses and provides indications of the ways in which the students were successful or unsuccessful in engaging with and completing the task. The descriptions are keyed to the *Core Elements of Performance*. Our global descriptions of student work range from "The student needs significant instruction" to "The student's work meets the essential demands of the task." Samples of student work that exemplify these descriptions of performance are included below, accompanied by commentary on central aspects of each student's response. These sample responses are *representative;* they may not mirror the global description of performance in all respects, being weaker in some and stronger in others.

The characterization of student responses for this task is based on these *Core Elements of Performance:*

1. Identify and define similar triangles.
2. Use scale factor of similar triangles to determine linear and area measures.
3. Use variables to represent 1- and 2-dimensional growth in similar triangles.

Descriptions of Student Work

The student needs significant instruction.

Student engages in the task but shows, at most, evidence of partial understanding of one of the two aspects of similarity being assessed in this task: (1) identifying and justifying which two figures are similar, and (2) identifying the effect of scale factor on both the linear and area measures of similar triangles. Note that simply identifying the correct triangle without adequate reasoning is only partial evidence of the first aspect. A partial understanding of the second aspect may be evidenced by appropriately using scale factors on specific lengths, but not on the area or for the generalizations (or vice versa).

Student A

Student A shows no evidence of understanding in either of the aspects. She fails to demonstrate that she understands the meaning of similar triangles.

She chooses the wrong triangle as similar to Triangle R and incorrectly uses various scale factors to find new heights, bases, and areas for triangles.

The student needs some instruction.

Student shows evidence of at least a partial understanding of both aspects of similarity: (1) identifying and justifying which two figures are similar, and (2) identifying the effect of scale factor on both the linear and area measures of similar triangles.

Student B

Student B shows evidence of partial understanding in the two aspects. First, Student B identifies the correct triangle similar to Triangle R and his explanation as to why they are similar is on the right track, though incomplete. For the second aspect, he correctly computes the heights and bases for similar triangles of a given scale factor. However, he is unsuccessful in determining the areas of triangles similar to R. It appears he finds the area by using the same method he used for finding height and base.

The student's work needs to be revised.

Student shows evidence of partial understanding in one aspect and adequate understanding of the other aspect of similarity being assessed in this task: (1) identifying and justifying which two figures are similar, and (2) identifying the effect of scale factor on both the linear and area measures of similar triangles. Note that an adequate understanding of the first aspect requires that the student select the correct similar triangle to Triangle R AND that the explanation be a reasonable way to determine the similarity (although it may lack some clarity). An adequate understanding of the second aspect would be evidence that the student knows to multiply by the scale factor to obtain the new lengths AND to multiply by the square of the scale factor to obtain the new area. (However, it is okay if the student does not take either of these all the way to a generalization.)

No student examples at this level.

The student's work meets the essential demands of the task.

Student shows evidence of adequate understanding in both aspects of similarity being assessed in this task: (1) identifying and justifying which two figures are similar, and (2) identifying the effect of scale factor on both the linear measure and area measure AND student generalizes for at least one of the two cases.

Task

10

Student C

Student C correctly identifies the triangle similar to Triangle R and provides a reasonable explanation for her approach. She also provides evidence of understanding the effect of scale factor on both length and area. Note that although she makes a mistake in the generalization for area, she is indeed multiplying by the square of the scale factor to find the area of the given specific cases.

Student D

Student D answers each question of the task correctly. Note that while the explanation of similarity in question 2 is incomplete (height and base being the same ratio is not adequate to ensure similarity), the student is working with right triangles, and it is likely that the student was assuming the right angle included between the two sides.

This problem gives you the chance to

■ *reason about similar figures and scale factor*

■ *generalize using variables*

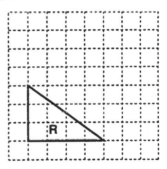

On your own

1. Which of the triangles below is similar to Triangle R?

Triangle #1

Triangle 1

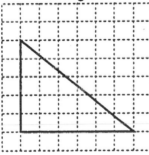

Triangle 2

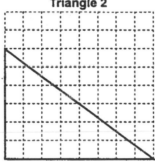

Triangle 3

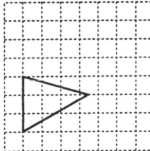

Triangle 4

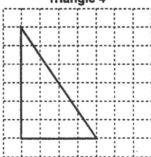

2. Describe how you decided which triangle was similar to R.

Well I took the one that looks exactly like it and was pretty much set on the graph the same way.

3. If Triangle R is enlarged, what will height and base lengths be for the new triangle for the following scale factors?

	Height	Base
scale factor of 2.5	2	1/2
scale factor of 10	5	5
scale factor of *n*	I don't	Know

4. If Triangle R is enlarged, what will the area be for the new triangle for the following scale factors?

scale factor of 2.5	1
scale factor of 10	5
scale factor of *n*	I don't Know

Student B

This problem gives you the chance to

■ *reason about similar figures and scale factor*

■ *generalize using variables*

On your own

1. Which of the triangles below is similar to Triangle R?

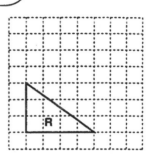

Triangle 1

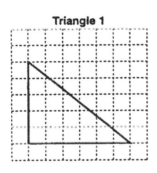

Triangle 2

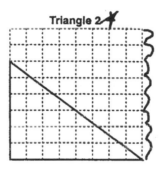

Triangle 3

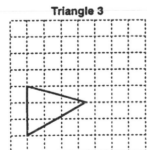

Triangle 4

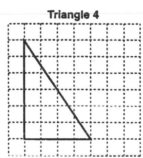

2. Describe how you decided which triangle was similar to R.

   Slopes are same   goes from 3/4 to 6/8

3. If Triangle R is enlarged, what will height and base lengths be for the new triangle for the following scale factors?

	Height	Base
scale factor of 2.5	7.5	10
scale factor of 10	30	40
scale factor of n	$3n$	$4n$

4. If Triangle R is enlarged, what will the area be for the new triangle for the following scale factors?

scale factor of 2.5	15
scale factor of 10	60
scale factor of n	$6n$

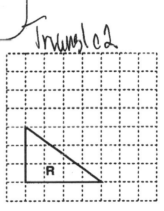

Triangle 2

This problem gives you the chance to

■ *reason about similar figures and scale factor*

■ *generalize using variables*

On your own

1. Which of the triangles below is similar to Triangle R?

Triangle 1

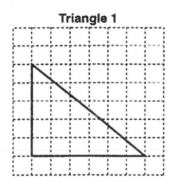

Triangle 2

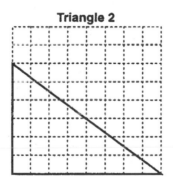

Triangle 3

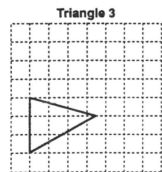

Triangle 4

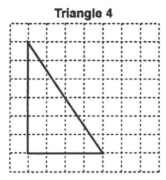

Student C

2. Describe how you decided which triangle was similar to R.

I fond the Scale factor of R
to all the other triangles & triangle
2 was similar with a scale factor of 2.

3. If Triangle R is enlarged, what will height and base lengths be for the new triangle for the following scale factors?

	Height	Base
scale factor of 2.5	7.5	10
scale factor of 10	30	40
scale factor of n	$3n$	$4n$

4. If Triangle R is enlarged, what will the area be for the new triangle for the following scale factors?

scale factor of 2.5	37.5
scale factor of 10	600
scale factor of n	$6n$

Student D

This problem gives you the chance to

■ *reason about similar figures and scale factor*

■ *generalize using variables 'es*

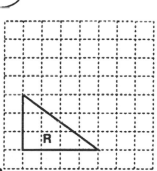

On your own

1. Which of the triangles below is similar to Triangle R?

Triangle 1

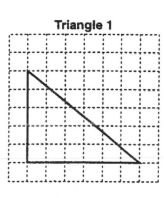

Triangle 2

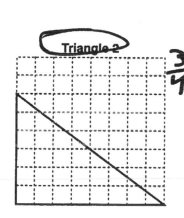

$$\frac{3}{4} = \frac{6}{8}$$

Triangle 3

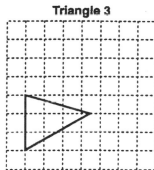

Triangle 4

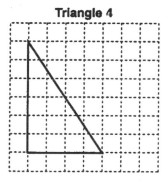

2. Describe how you decided which triangle was similar to R.

The ratio of the height and base is the same for triangle R and triangle 2

3. If Triangle R is enlarged, what will height and base lengths be for the new triangle for the following scale factors?

	Height	Base
scale factor of 2.5	7.5	10
scale factor of 10	30	40
scale factor of n	$3n$	$4n$

4. If Triangle R is enlarged, what will the area be for the new triangle for the following scale factors?

scale factor of 2.5   37.5

scale factor of 10   600

scale factor of n $\dfrac{3n(4n)}{2}$

Produce sets of numbers that result in given decimal totals.

Disk Sum Problem

Short Task

Task Description

The student is given four sums and a picture of two 2-sided disks that are blank on each side. The student has to find four numbers and assign one for each side of each disk. When the disks are flipped, the sum of the numbers of the sides facing up must yield one of the four given sums.

Assumed Mathematical Background

It is assumed that students have a background in decimal addition.

Core Elements of Performance

- add decimals accurately
- find at least two sets of rational numbers that satisfy the problem's constraints

Circumstances

Grouping:	Students complete an individual written response.
Materials:	No special materials are needed for this task.
Estimated time:	25 minutes

Disk Sum Problem

This problem gives you the chance to

- *add decimals accurately*
- *find numbers that produce given sums*

Here are 2 blank disks.

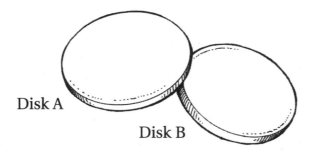

Disk A

Disk B

1. Sara chose four numbers and wrote one number on each side of the two disks above. She said that if she flipped the disks and added the two numbers that were facing up, the sum was always one of the following numbers: 0.1, 0.23, 0.87, or 1. Find the numbers that Sara could have placed on each face of Disk A and Disk B. (Show your work clearly.)

2. John found a solution but all four of his numbers were different from those Sara found. When John and Sara compared solutions they found that one solution set contained the number zero and the other solution set did not.

Find another solution set to this problem in addition to the one you found for question 1. Of your two solution sets for questions 1 and 2, one should contain the number zero and the other should not.

Task

A Sample Solution

If students limit themselves to positive numbers, the following solutions are some of the many that are possible. (The number of possible answers is infinite.)

Given Sums: **0.1, 0.23, 0.87, 1**

Sample Solutions:

| Disk A: 0.13 | 0 | Disk A: 0.22 | 0.09 |
| Disk B: 0.87 | 0.1 | Disk B: 0.78 | 0.01 |

| Disk A: 0.80 | 0.03 | Disk A: 0.23 | 0.1 |
| Disk B: 0.20 | 0.07 | Disk B: 0.77 | 0 |

If students use negative numbers, then additional solutions are possible, such as the ones listed below.

Given Sums: **0.1, 0.23, 0.87, 1**

Sample Solutions:

| Disk A: 0.115 | 0.885 | Disk A: 0.46 | 0.33 |
| Disk B: 0.115 | -0.015 | Disk B: 0.54 | -0.23 |

NOTE: Students are likely to use trial and error. They must realize that to come to a correct solution, the numbers that share a disk cannot be added to one another to produce one of the needed sums.

More on the Mathematics

If Disk A has sides with numbers a and b, and Disk B has sides with numbers c and d, then one workable set of sums is

(1) $a + c = 1$ This implies that $c = 1 - a$

(2) $a + d = 0.87$ This implies that $d = 0.87 - a$

(3) $b + c = 0.23$ This implies that $b = 0.23 - c$, and using (1), $b = a - 0.77$

(4) $b + d = 0.1$ This implies that $b = 0.1 - d$, and using (2), $b = a - 0.77$

It is possible to choose any value for a and then find values for b, c, and d which suit the required conditions, since there are in effect only three independent equations. For instance, adding equations (2) and (3) and subtracting equation (1) gives equation (4).

Some examples of the many solutions:

a	b	c	d
1	0.23	0	- 0.13
0.87	0.1	0.13	0
0.83	0.06	0.17	0.04
0.82	0.05	0.18	0.05
0.85	0.08	0.15	0.02

Task

Using this Task

11

Review with students the aims of the assessment listed in the box at the top of the first activity page. Read the task with the students. Answer any questions that have to do with understanding the task. If students ask questions on how to begin, refer them back to the questions posed.

Characterizing Performance

This section offers a characterization of student responses and provides indications of the ways in which the students were successful or unsuccessful in engaging with and completing the task. The descriptions are keyed to the *Core Elements of Performance*. Our global descriptions of student work range from "The student needs significant instruction" to "The student's work meets the essential demands of the task." Samples of student work that exemplify these descriptions of performance are included below, accompanied by commentary on central aspects of each student's response. These sample responses are *representative*; they may not mirror the global description of performance in all respects, being weaker in some and stronger in others.

The characterization of student responses for this task is based on these *Core Elements of Performance:*
1. Add decimals accurately.
2. Find at least two sets of rational numbers that satisfy the problem's constraints.

Descriptions of Student Work

The student needs significant instruction.

Student shows evidence of understanding that sums of two numbers give the totals of 0.1, 0.23, 0.87, and 1. While the student may show evidence of totaling pairs of numbers in an attempt to make these totals, no solution for disk labels is found.

Student A

Student A exhibits an understanding that sums of two numbers give the totals being sought. However, the pairs of numbers that are added together to give each of the sums do not show evidence of finding one set of four disk labels that can be combined to produce the four given sums.

The student needs some instruction.

Student finds one partial solution, showing numbers that would produce at least three of the given sums.

Student B

While Student B's first solution has numbers that can potentially result in the given totals, the assumed pairing on the disks (0.8 and 0.2 on Disk A, 0.03 and 0.07 on Disk B) result in two sums that are appropriate and two that are not: $0.8 + 0.03 = 0.83$ and $0.2 + 0.07 = 0.27$. Since the student does not provide any indications for which numbers to pair, there is no evidence of a full solution. The second solution has two major errors: the assumed pairing of the addends doesn't correspond to what can potentially be used on the disks. Also, there is an addition error in the final addition sentence: $0.87 + 0.23 = 1.1$; not 1 as indicated by the student.

The student's work needs to be revised.

Student finds one full and one partial solution (for example, student may produce a second correct set, but neither set includes a zero; or student may find a second solution that produces only three of the totals).

Student C

Student C finds only one set of possible addends, which she labels A1, A2, B1, B2. Student C's work suggests that she found four addends that would produce sums that are each 100 times what is needed. After finding these addends she took 0.01 of each of them and produced the decimal numbers. She appears to use the same strategy with three sets of numbers. Her response is lacking clarity and it does not indicate which (if any) of the sets is a possible solution.

The student's work meets the essential demands of the task.

Student correctly produces two full solutions to the problem, one including a zero and the other not. The student may not have indicated which number belongs on which disk, and may not have indicated a check of all the sums.

Student D

Student D finds two sets of addends that produce the needed sums and correctly indicates which addends must be paired together to produce the needed sums.

$$A1 + B1 = 1$$
$$A1 + B2 = .23$$
$$A2 + B2 = .87$$
$$A2 + B1 = .1$$

$1 (.25 + .75)$

$(.5 + .5)$

$(.3 + .7)$

$(.4 + .6)$

$(.2 + .8)$

$(.9 + .1)$

$.23 (.115 + .115)$

$(.2 + .03)$

$(.1 + .13)$

$.87 (.8 + .07)$

$(.435 + .435)$

$(.2 + .67)$

$(.1 + .77)$

$.1 (.05 + .05)$

1. Sara placed one number on each side of the two disks above. She said that if she flipped the disks and added the two numbers that were facing up, the sum was always one of the following numbers: 0.1, 0.23, 0.87, or 1.
   Find the numbers that Sara could have placed on each face of disk A and disk B. (Show your work clearly.)

   .8
   .2
   .03
   .07

2. John found a solution but all four of his numbers were different from those Sara found. When John and Sara compared solutions they found that one solution set contained the number zero and the other solution set did not.
   Find another solution set to this problem in addition to the one you found for question 1. Of your two solution sets for questions 1 and 2, one should contain the number zero and the other should not.

   .0   0+.23=.23
   .87   6+.87=.87
   .23   6+.1=.1
   .1   .87+.23= 1

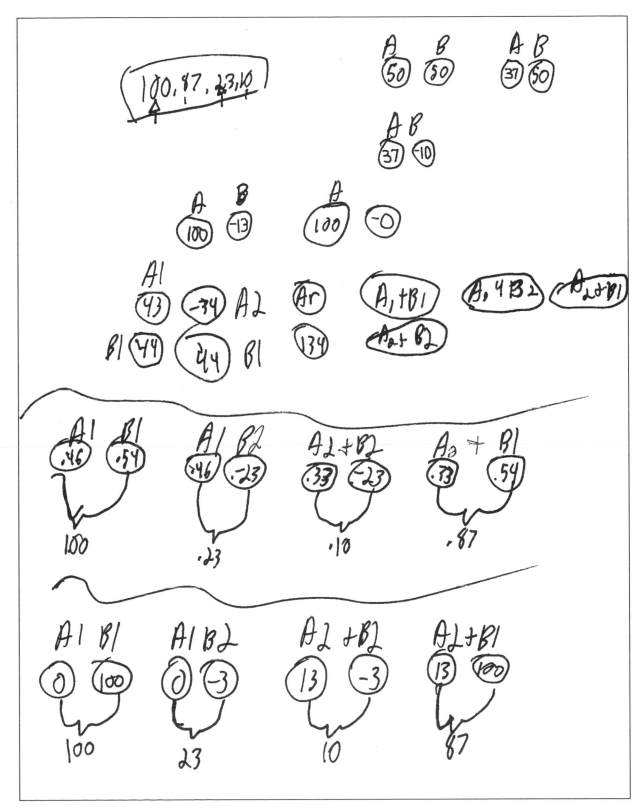

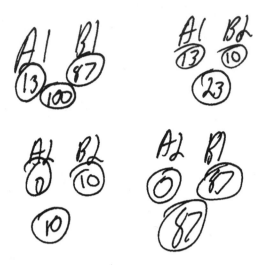

1. Sara placed one number on each side of the two disks above. She said that if she flipped the disks and added the two numbers that were facing up, the sum was always one of the following numbers: 0.1, 0.23, 0.87, or 1.

   Find the numbers that Sara could have placed on each face of disk A and disk B. (Show your work clearly.)

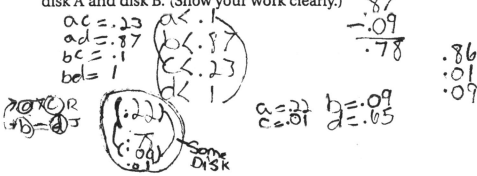

2. John found a solution but all four of his numbers were different from those Sara found. When John and Sara compared solutions they found that one solution set contained the number zero and the other solution set did not.

Find another solution set to this problem in addition to the one you found for question 1. Of your two solution sets for questions 1 and 2, one should contain the number zero and the other should not.

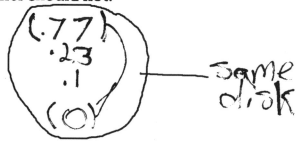

12

Stacking Cubes

Use spatial reasoning to
represent and find the
volume and surface area
of stacks of cubes.

Short Task

Task Description

Students are given the corner view of stacks of cubes. Using spatial visualization skills they must determine the maximum number of cubes that could be used to make the stacks, represent the stacks on grid paper, and find the surface area of the stacks.

Assumed Mathematical Background

It is assumed that students have had experience representing 3-dimensional objects on isometric dot and square grid paper and arc familiar with volume and surface area measures of objects.

Core Elements of Performance

- use spatial reasoning to determine the maximum number of cubes that could be used to make the figure

- use grid paper to represent the base (squares that would be covered by the bottom of the figure) of the maximum figure

- use spatial reasoning to determine the surface area of the maximum figure

Circumstances

Grouping:	Students complete an individual written response.
Materials:	interlocking cubes (at least 15 per student), isometric dot paper, and square grid paper
Estimated time:	15 minutes

Stacking Cubes

Stacking Cubes

This problem gives you the chance to

- *use spatial reasoning*
- *represent the stacks of cubes on grid paper*
- *determine the maximum number of cubes needed to build the 3-D figure*
- *find surface area*

This is an isometric drawing of a corner view of a building model made with interlocking cubes. (You may want to use some cubes to make the structure.)

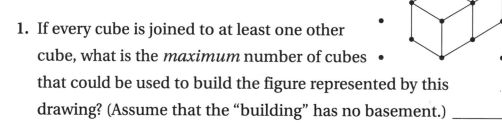

1. If every cube is joined to at least one other cube, what is the *maximum* number of cubes that could be used to build the figure represented by this drawing? (Assume that the "building" has no basement.) _____

2. If you build the figure above using the maximum number of cubes, lightly fill in the squares on the grid that would be covered by the bottom of the figure.

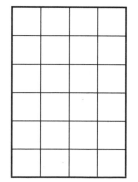

3. Write a number in each square you shaded in question 2 to represent the number of cubes that would be stacked above that square.

4. If you were to glue the cubes of the maximum figure together and paint the surface (including the bottom), what would be the area that you painted? Describe how you found your answer.

Task 12 **A Sample Solution**

1. 7 cubes. The five cubes shown and an additional 2 blocked from view by the stack of 3 cubes.

2.

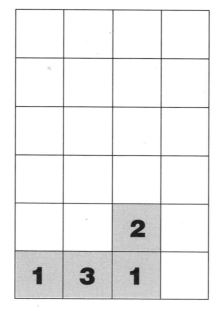

3.

		2	
1	**3**	**1**	

4. Based on a correct answer of 7 cubes in question 1.

Top and Bottom View	4 squares each	8 squares total
Front and Back View	6 squares each	12 squares total
Side Views	5 squares each	10 squares total
Total Surface Area		30

Partial credit is given for stating that 8 cubes could be in the drawing (some students may add an unconnected cube in the diagonal behind the 2-high stack). The surface area for this drawing is:

Top and Bottom View	5 squares each	10 squares total
Front and Back View	7 squares each	14 squares total
Side Views	6 squares each	12 squares total
Total Surface Area		36

For students who identify only 6 cubes in the drawing the surface area of that figure is:

Top and Bottom View	4 squares each	8 squares total
Front and Back View	5 squares each	10 squares total
Side Views	4 squares each	8 squares total
Total Surface Area		26

For students who identify only 5 cubes in the drawing, the surface area of that figure is:

Top and Bottom View	3 squares each	6 squares total
Front and Back View	5 squares each	10 squares total
Side Views	3 squares each	6 squares total
Total Surface Area		22

Task

Using this Task

Each student will require a copy of the task. Cubes should be available for those students who want to build the stacks of cubes. Teachers should either have cubes available and allow students to decide how many they need or have them packaged in bags of 15 to 20.

Because this task is short and straightforward, it would be appropriate simply to hand out the task and direct students to read and answer the questions individually.

Issues for Classroom Use

This problem is small and very contained, provided that students have had experiences with representing 3-dimensional objects on isometric dot paper and square grid paper and have looked for maximum situations. Students may have trouble visualizing that a total of 2 cubes could be hidden behind the 3-high tower. This shows lack of a robust understanding of the limits of 2-dimensional drawings to represent 3-dimensional objects. Some students can visualize only what is directly in the drawing. Students who have trouble with this task need additional experiences with spatial reasoning and investigating representations of 3-dimensional objects.

Characterizing Performance

This section offers a characterization of student responses and provides indications of the ways in which the students were successful or unsuccessful in engaging with and completing the task. The descriptions are keyed to the *Core Elements of Performance*. Our global descriptions of student work range from "The student needs significant instruction" to "The student's work meets the essential demands of the task." Samples of student work that exemplify these descriptions of performance are included below, accompanied by commentary on central aspects of each student's response. These sample responses are *representative;* they may not mirror the global description of performance in all respects, being weaker in some and stronger in others.

The characterization of student responses for this task is based on these *Core Elements of Performance:*

1. Use spatial reasoning to determine the maximum number of cubes that could be used to make the figure.
2. Use grid paper to represent the base (squares that would be covered by the bottom of the figure) of the maximum figure.
3. Use spatial reasoning to determine the surface area of the maximum figure.

Descriptions of Student Work

The student needs significant instruction.

Student provides no evidence of recognizing there are hidden cubes in the isometric drawing. There is no evidence of understanding the meaning of a base view representation (squares that would be covered by the bottom of the figure) OR the meaning of surface area.

Student A

Student A's answer of "5" to question 1 indicates that he does not recognize that there are hidden cubes. For question 2 he has represented an outline of the structure he sees, not its base (squares that would be covered by the bottom of the figure). The numbers on the drawing appear to be simply a count of the number of cubes in the structure. Surface area is incorrect.

Task

The student needs some instruction.

Student provides no evidence of recognizing there are hidden cubes in the isometric drawing. But there is evidence of understanding the meaning of a base view representation (squares that would be covered by the bottom of the figure) AND/OR of the meaning of surface area. While there is evidence of some consistency in the number of cubes across the questions, there may be some counting and calculation errors.

Student B

Student B's answer of "9" for the maximum number of cubes seems to indicate that she realizes there are hidden cubes. However, none of her subsequent work supports this idea. Her base view (squares that would be covered by the bottom of the figure) indicates some understanding of representing the figure, but she shows no hidden cubes. She finds a surface area that is consistent with her base view.

The student's work needs to be revised.

Student successfully identifies 1 hidden cube. Alternatively, student may have identified 8 cubes—that is, the 7 actual cubes plus one that is (contrary to the directions) unattached to the rest of the building but which is in fact hidden from view. In either case, student shows evidence of understanding the meaning of a base view representation AND of the meaning of surface area. While there is evidence of consistency across questions, there may be some counting and calculation errors.

No student examples at this level.

The student's work meets the demand of the task.

Student successfully identifies 7 cubes as the maximum and indicates it in the base view (squares that would be covered by the bottom of the figure) of the figure in question 2. There is evidence of understanding the meaning of a base view representation AND of the meaning of surface area. While there is evidence of consistency across questions, there may be some counting and calculation errors.

Student C

Student C correctly states the maximum number of cubes that makes up the isometric representation as 7. She shows the squares that would be covered by the bottom of the figure and the correct number of cubes in each stack for a figure of 7 cubes. She correctly calculates and describes how she found the total surface area for the 7-cube figure.

Student A

This problem gives you the chance to

- *use spatial reasoning*
- *represent the stacks of cubes on grid paper*
- *determine the maximum number of cubes needed to build the 3-D figure*
- *find surface area*

This is an isometric drawing of a corner view of a building model made with interlocking cubes. (You may want to use some cubes to make the structure.)

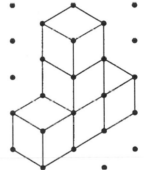

1. If every cube is joined to at least one other cube, what is the *maximum* number of cubes that could be used to build the figure represented by this drawing? (Assume that the "building" has no basement.) _____

   5

2. If you build the figure above using the maximum number of cubes, lightly fill in the squares on the grid that would be covered by the bottom of the figure.

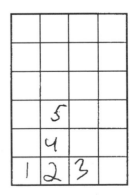

3. Write a number in each square you shaded in question 2 to represent the number of cubes that would be stacked above that square.

4. If you were to glue the cubes of the maximum figure together and paint the surface (including the bottom), what would be the area that you painted? Describe how you found your answer.   5 I counted the sides,

This problem gives you the chance to

- *use spatial reasoning*
- *represent the stacks of cubes on grid paper*
- *determine the maximum number of cubes needed to build the 3-D figure*
- *find surface area*

This is an isometric drawing of a corner view of a building model made with **interlocking** cubes. (You may want to use some cubes to make the structure.)

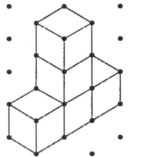

1. If every cube is joined to at least one other cube, what is the *maximum* number of cubes that could be used to build the figure represented by this drawing? (Assume that the "building" has no basement.) _____9_____

   The maximum number of cubes is 9.

2. If you build the figure above using the maximum number of cubes, lightly fill in the squares on the grid that would be covered by the bottom of the figure.

3. Write a number in each square you shaded in question 2 to represent the number of cubes that would be stacked above that square.

4. If you were to glue the cubes of the maximum figure together and paint the surface (including the bottom), what would be the area that you painted? Describe how you found your answer.

The area I painted would be 22. I found this by counting each surface area I could see twice.

Student C

This problem gives you the chance to

- *use spatial reasoning*
- *represent the stacks of cubes on grid paper*
- *determine the maximum number of cubes needed to build the 3-D figure*
- *find surface area*

This is an isometric drawing of a corner view of a building model made with interlocking cubes. (You may want to use some cubes to make the structure.)

1. If every cube is joined to at least one other cube, what is the *maximum* number of cubes that could be used to build the figure represented by this drawing? (Assume that the "building" has no basement.) _____

   7 cubes is the maximum.

2. If you build the figure above using the maximum number of cubes, lightly fill in the squares on the grid that would be covered by the bottom of the figure.

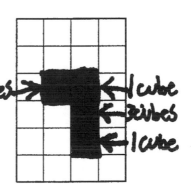

2 cubes → ← 1 cube
← 3 cubes
← 1 cube

3. Write a number in each square you shaded in question 2 to represent the number of cubes that would be stacked above that square.

4. If you were to glue the cubes of the maximum figure together and paint the surface (including the bottom), what would be the area that you painted? Describe how you found your answer.

30 squints

To find this answer I counted all the blocks on the outside surface.

13

Drop and Bounce

> Represent an exponential function in a table, as a graph, and as an algebraic expression.

Short Task

Task Description

This task uses the context of a ball that rises to half its previous height each time it bounces. Students are asked to determine the number of times the ball will bounce before it peaks at a certain height. They are asked to represent this situation in a table, as a graph, and as an algebraic expression.

Assumed Mathematical Background

It is assumed that students who have had experience representing functions in tables and graphs should be able to engage in the first three questions in this task. Question 4 may be challenging for students who have not had experiences representing exponential functions algebraically.

Core Elements of Performance

- determine the number of times a ball bounces to reach a specific peak height
- represent a discrete exponential function in a table, as a graph, and as an algebraic expression

Circumstances

Grouping:	Students complete an individual written response.
Materials:	No special materials are needed for this task.
Estimated time:	20 minutes

Drop and Bounce

This problem gives you the chance to

- *interpret a situation*
- *represent a function as a table, a graph, and an algebraic expression*

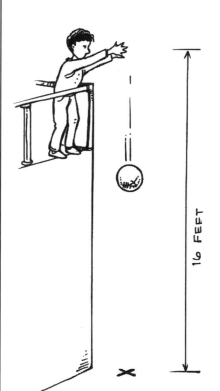

16 FEET

A ball is dropped from a height of 16 feet. At its first bounce, the ball reaches a peak height of 8 feet. Each successive time that the ball bounces, it reaches a peak height that is half that of the bounce just before.

1. How many times will the ball bounce until it bounces to a peak height of 1 foot? Show how you found your answer.

2. Make a table that shows the peak bounce height of the ball for each number of bounces.

3. Make a graph that shows the relationship between the number of bounces and the peak height of the ball.

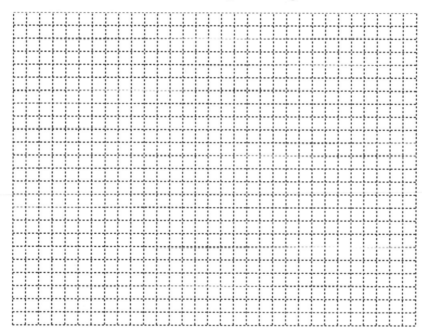

4. Write an algebraic expression that shows the relationship between the number of bounces and the peak height of the ball.

Task **A Sample Solution**

1. 4 bounces. I found this by looking at the table below.

2.

Number of bounces	Height of ball at top of bounce
0	16 feet
1	8 feet
2	4 feet
3	2 feet
4	1 feet
5	0.5 feet
6	0.25 feet

3.

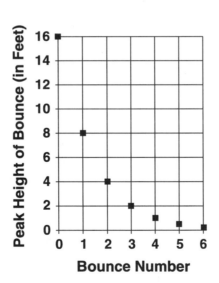

4. For b = number of bounces, h = peak height of bounce

$h = 2^{(4 - b)}$

OR

$h = \frac{16}{2^b}$

OR an equivalent expression.

Using this Task

Review the aims of the assessment in the box at the top of the first activity page. Read the problem aloud to your students. Because this task is short and straightforward, it would be appropriate simply to hand out the task and leave students to individually read and answer the questions.

Issues for Classroom Use

Most middle grade students should be able to successfully complete questions 1 through 3 of this task. Question 4 asks students to write an exponential function in symbolic form. This may be difficult for students who have not had prior experiences with such tasks. However, in such cases you may still wish to assess students' knowledge of functions by having them answer questions 1 through 3 and using question 4 as a special challenge.

Task

Characterizing Performance

13

This section offers a characterization of student responses and provides indications of the ways in which the students were successful or unsuccessful in engaging with and completing the task. The descriptions are keyed to the *Core Elements of Performance.* Our global descriptions of student work range from "The student needs significant instruction" to "The student's work meets the essential demands of the task." Samples of student work that exemplify these descriptions of performance are included below, accompanied by commentary on central aspects of each student's response. These sample responses are *representative;* they may not mirror the global description of performance in all respects, being weaker in some and stronger in others.

The characterization of student responses for this task is based on these *Core Elements of Performance:*

1. Determine the number of times a ball bounces to reach a specific peak height.
2. Represent a discrete exponential function in a table, as a graph, and as an algebraic expression.

Descriptions of Student Work

The student needs significant instruction.

Student correctly determines the number of bounces to arrive at a specific peak height, but does not successfully complete other parts of the problem.

No student examples at this level.

The student needs some instruction.

Student correctly determines the number of bounces and represents the information accurately in one representation: a table, a graph, or an equation.

Student A

Student A successfully completes questions 1 and 2 of the task, although he does not include the decimal in the bounce height after the fifth bounce. While his reasoning is not evident from his response to question 1, it can be inferred from his table. Student A attempts a graph but does not make appropriate use of scale, which indicates a serious problem in using graphs to represent functions. The given equation is incorrect if one infers that the variables represent bounce height and number of bounces.

The student's work needs to be revised.

Student correctly determines the number of bounces and represents the information in two forms, providing evidence of understanding the two representations. There is consistency among the representations and the situation. (Some minor errors are okay.)

Student B

Student B correctly answers questions 1 and 2. On question 3 her initial graph plotting the points is accurate and complete. She has used a table and graph to correctly represent the number of bounces and the corresponding bounce height. Note that her sketch of a line on the graph suggests she is searching for a line of best fit to describe the graph with an equation, indicating that she does not consider or is not familiar with exponential functions. However, she does correctly realize that a linear function cannot accurately represent this situation.

Student C

Student C answers all questions correctly, with some minor errors. The student connects the points on the graph, implying a continuous function. This inaccurately represents the situation since a ball can bounce only a whole number of times (there is no 1.2 number of bounces). Student C fails to label the axes of the graph and indicate what x and y represent. The student's equation is correct, if you assume x is the number of bounces and y is the peak height. (Note: some curricula use "^" to symbolize "to the power of.")

The student's work meets the essential demands of the task.

Student answers questions 1 through 4 correctly and completely with only minor errors.

Student D

Student D answers all questions completely and correctly.

This problem gives you the chance to

- *interpret a situation*
- *represent a function as a table, a graph, and an algebraic expression*

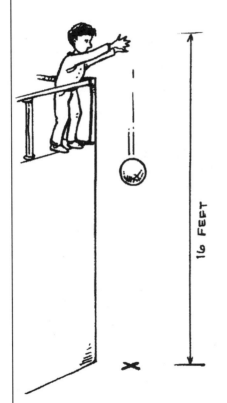

16 FEET

A ball is dropped from a height of 16 feet. At its first bounce, the ball reaches a peak height of 8 feet. Each successive time that the ball bounces, it reaches a peak height that is half that of the bounce just before.

1. How many times will the ball bounce until it bounces to a peak height of 1 foot? Show how you found your answer.

4 times   16
            8
            4
            2
            1

Student A

2. Make a table that shows the peak bounce height of the ball for each number of bounces.

BH	16	8	4	2	1	.5
NofB	0	1	2	3	4	5

3. Make a graph that shows the relationship between the number of bounces and the peak height of the ball.

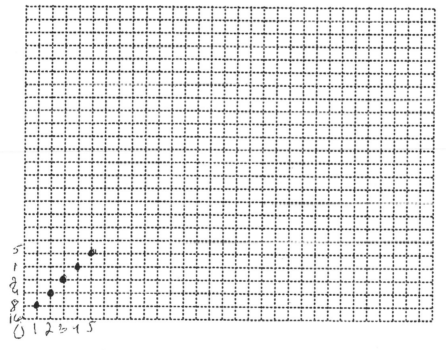

4. Write an algebraic expression that shows the relationship between the number of bounces and the peak height of the ball.

$$y = \frac{1}{2} \times B$$

This problem gives you the chance to

- *interpret a situation*
- *represent a function as a table, a graph, and an algebraic expression*

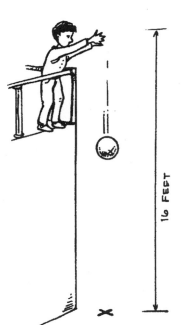

A ball is dropped from a height of 16 feet. At its first bounce, the ball reaches a peak height of 8 feet. Each successive time that the ball bounces, it reaches a peak height that is half that of the bounce just before.

1. How many times will the ball bounce until it bounces to a peak height of 1 foot? Show how you found your answer.

Bounces	1	2	3	4
Height	8	4	2	1

÷2   ÷2   ÷2

The ball would have to bounce 4 times for the peak height to be 1 foot.

2. Make a table that shows the peak bounce height of the ball for the number of bounces.

Bounces	Peak Height
	0 ft
1	8 ft
2	4 ft
3	2 ft
4	1 ft
5	0.5 ft
6	0.25"

3. Make a graph that shows the relationship between the number of bounces and the peak height of the ball.

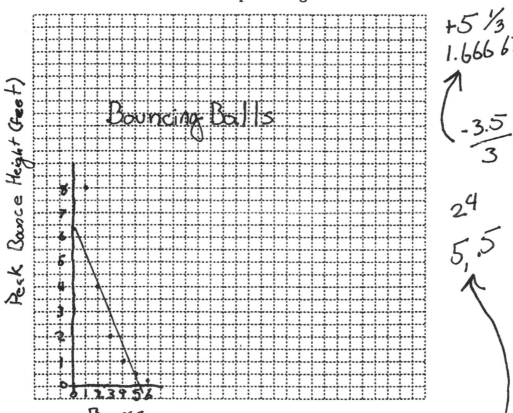

Bouncing Balls

Peak Bounce Height (feet)

Bounce

+5 ⅓
1.666 67

-3.5
3

2⁴

5,5

4. Write an algebraic expression that shows the relationship between the number of bounces and the peak height of the ball.

I cannot find an equation to fit data-line of best fit is I dont know I cant find it

Student C

This problem gives you the chance to

■ *interpret a situation*
■ *represent a function as a table, a graph, and an algebraic expression*

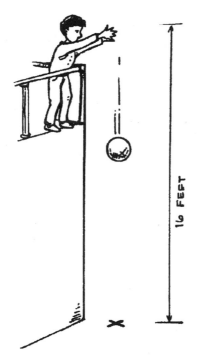

16 FEET

A ball is dropped from a height of 16 feet. At its first bounce, the ball reaches a peak height of 8 feet. Each successive time that the ball bounces, it reaches a peak height that is half that of the bounce just before.

1. How many times will the ball bounce until it bounces to a peak height of 1 foot? Show how you found your answer.

$16 \div 2 = \textcircled{8} \div 2 = \textcircled{4} \div 2 = \textcircled{2} \div 2 = 1 \, Ft$

4 Bounces

Got it From table And Division Statement

2. Make a table that shows the peak bounce height of the ball for each number of bounces.

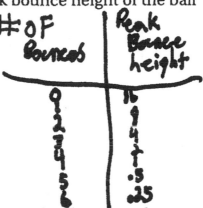

3. Make a graph that shows the relationship between the number of bounces and the peak height of the ball.

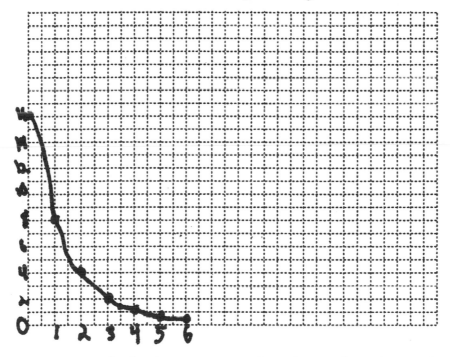

4. Write an algebraic expression that shows the relationship between the number of bounces and the peak height of the ball.

$$y = 16 \div 2\,\hat{}\,x$$

This problem gives you the chance to

- *interpret a situation*
- *represent a function as a table, a graph, and an algebraic expression*

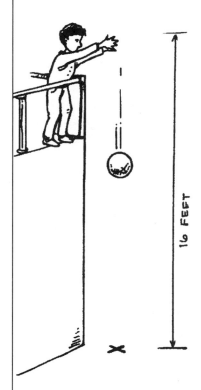

16 FEET

A ball is dropped from a height of 16 feet. At its first bounce, the ball reaches a peak height of 8 feet. Each successive time that the ball bounces, it reaches a peak height that is half that of the bounce just before.

1. How many times will the ball bounce until it bounces to a peak height of 1 foot? Show how you found your answer. 4 bounces

I took 16 and divided it by 2 (half), and ended up with 8. That was 1 bounce. Then, I took 8 and divided it by 2, and ended up with 4. 2 bounces. I then proceeded to divide 4 by 2, with an answer of 2. That was three bounces. Then, on the fourth bounce, I took 2 divided by 2 and came up with

2. Make a table that shows the peak bounce height of the ball for the number of bounces.

bounces	height
0	16
1	8
2	4
3	2
4	1
5	.5
6	.25
7	.125

3. Make a graph that shows the relationship between the number of bounces and the peak height of the ball.

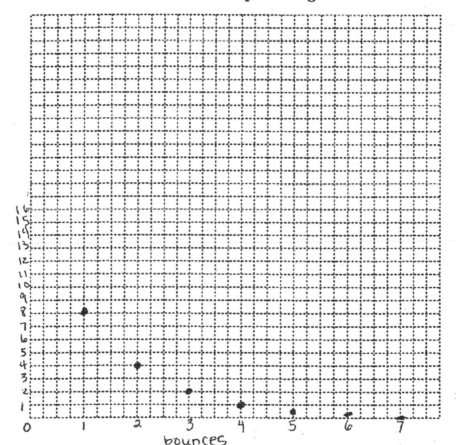

4. Write an algebraic expression that shows the relationship between the number of bounces and the peak height of the ball.

h = height
b = bounces

$$h = 16 \div 2^b$$

14

Parachutes

Design a game.
Collect and use
experimental data.
Justify decisions.
Pose questions.

Extended Task

Task Description

Students give advice on how to design a parachutes carnival game that is
both fun and profitable. Based on their experimental data and knowledge of
probability, they include information on constructing the game, rules, prizes,
cost to play, and so on.

Assumed Mathematical Background

It is assumed that students have had experience conducting investigations
using experimental probability and in analyzing their data. Students are also
expected to be familiar with geometric ideas, such as constructing circles and
measurement.

Core Elements of Performance

- design a game within given parameters with clear and consistent rules
- collect and organize experimental data
- analyze data
- interpret data to modify rules for a game
- formulate further questions
- communicate mathematical reasoning in support of choices

Circumstances

Grouping:	Following a class introduction, students work in groups to complete a written response.
Materials:	large sheets of newsprint, felt-tip markers, 3"-by-5" index cards, tape, scissors, string, and paper clips
Estimated time:	180 minutes

Parachutes

This problem gives you the chance to

- *design a parachutes game with clear and consistent rules*

- *collect, organize, and interpret data*

- *communicate mathematical arguments in support of your conclusions*

- *formulate further questions*

As a class

A class is planning to run several games for the school fair to earn money for a class computer. After brainstorming many types of games as a class, your group has been chosen to work on the "Parachutes" game. The class has already decided on the following ideas:

- The parachutes are made from 3"-by-5" index cards.

- Players stand on a chair and drop a parachute, attempting to make it land in the center of a target on the floor.

- The target has 5 rings. Players earn points according to where the parachute lands: 5 points for the center, 4 points for the next ring, then 3 points, 2 points, and finally, 1 point for the outermost ring.

- Players pay for a turn to drop parachutes. They win different prizes depending on their total scores.

In small groups

Your assignment is to develop the details of this game so that it is fun and makes a profit, and people feel they have a chance at winning. Your group's **Final Report** to the class should include the following sections:

I. The Game

a. **The Parachute:** Include an example and a clear description of how to make the parachutes and explain why you think this is a good design.

b. **The Target:** Include an example and a clear description of how to make the target and explain why you think it is a good size for the game.

c. **The Rules:** Include a clear set of rules with details on the height of the chair, from what height the parachute should be dropped, the cost to play the game, costs of the prizes, and so on.

II. The Data

a. **Results:** Present the data you collected that helped you make decisions about the game's design. Make sure your data are well organized and easy to understand.

b. **Interpretation:** Discuss how you used the data to make your decisions about the game's design and how the data support those decisions.

III. Reflections

Identify at least 3 issues, problems, or questions that need further investigation in designing the best parachute game possible. Provide evidence to illustrate why the questions posed will be important in refining or modifying the game.

A Sample Solution

This task is designed to be very open-ended and allow for multiple reasonable solutions. A complete solution must address each portion of the **Final Report** guidelines in full and meet the *Core Elements of Performance*. A description of what students should include in each section follows.

I. The Game
a. The Parachute:
The description of how to make the parachute should include words and/or diagrams that would enable someone to reconstruct the parachute. Students should justify their choice of a parachute design. A response could simply say that the parachute lands in different spots and one cannot predict where it will land. Or students could include data gathered from a number of different parachute designs and use the data as an explanation of why their choice of parachute makes the best sense for the game. For example, students may wish to choose a parachute that does not consistently land in the center in order to make a profit, but that does occasionally yield a win, so that people will continue to play.

b. The Target:
The description of how to make the target should include words and/or diagrams that would enable someone to reconstruct the target. Students should also include some explanation of their choice of target size. This could be a simple statement such as how the difference in the diameters of the concentric circles is related to the size of the parachute or a reasoned explanation based on analysis of experimental data.

c. The Rules:
The rules should include information on all the requested elements: height of the chair, from what height the parachute should be dropped, the cost to play the game, costs of the prizes. The rules should also allow someone to reconstruct the exact conditions of the game. Good student solutions often include other details, such as: distance of the target from the chair, height of player's arm, and so on. The rules can be set before experimental data is collected, or students may choose to collect some data, modify the rules, and then collect additional data.

II. The Data

a. Results:

Students may choose to collect data that helps them make decisions about each of the three sections in **The Game**—parachute, target, and rules—but this is not expected. It is expected that students will collect data that will help them determine the cost to play and cost of prizes in order to make a profit. Students may not be satisfied with the predicted profit for this game based on their data (it may not seem to be enough to purchase a computer) or they may decide that the game cannot make a profit as designed and requires a major overhaul. Regardless, students should show consideration of the cost/profit issue, collect experimental data designed to inform decisions on this issue, display the data clearly, and correctly compute a predicted profit or profit margin per play. A full solution should include a large number of trials, such as at least 100 parachute drops.

b. Interpretation:

As in **Results**, students may collect and interpret data to inform many decisions, but they *must* collect and interpret data to inform decisions about cost to play the game, points needed to win a prize, and cost of prizes. Interpretation includes: calculation of predicted profit, judgment as to profitability of game, and redesign of costs involved so that profit is possible (if necessary).

III. Reflections

This section asks for students to identify three issues that require further investigation to design the best parachute game possible and to justify their choices. Students may discuss a need to do additional investigation (for example, actual costs of prizes), or to do additional experimentation with certain aspects of the game, to know more about the carnival (age of attendees, number of expected attendees, other games that will be there, environmental conditions, etc.); and students may raise issues about their inability to predict exactly what will happen in the actual carnival.

Task **Using this Task**

1. Organize the class into small groups of 2 or 3. Each group will need a chair (to stand on) and some space around the chair.

2. Have the students create their parachutes from a 3"-by-5" index card. Shown here is an example of how a parachute could be made.

Students may try variations on this design such as cutting the card smaller or using different kinds of cuts.

3. With the students, read the general description of the game at the bottom of the first student page entitled, *As a class.* Discuss this with students to ensure they understand the context of the task.

4. Review with students the aim of this assessment in the box at the top of the page. Review the students' assignment on the next page. Answer any questions students have about *what* they are supposed to do. Leave all decisions as to *how* to go about the task to the students. You may wish to remind them that they will need to justify the decisions they make (parachute design, target design, cost to play, cost of prizes, and so on).

Issues for Classroom Use

This task relies heavily on students' collecting and analyzing experimental data. For example, students may first design a target and a parachute and then test it a small number of times. Should the students find that the parachute consistently lands in the center of the target, this may cause them to modify part of their design of the game (such as the parachute, the target, the height of the player's arm, and so on). Students should keep track of this data and use it in their report as justification for the decisions that they made.

Students' analysis of their experimental data is often crucial in making decisions about cost and profit. (Students may choose to give prizes only to the top winners of the game in the fair and thereby eliminate much of the need to conduct an income/expense analysis of their experimental data.) Suppose students decide that players will pay $1.50 for a turn to drop three parachutes and assign prizes as follows:

Points player earns	Prize and estimated cost
13–15	Giant stuffed penguin: $12.00
10–12	Medium stuffed mouse: $7.50
7–9	Toy watch: $5.00
4–6	Dwarf doll: $2.00
less than 4	No prize

Then the students collect data like the following, based on 50 turns of playing the game:

# of points	0–2	3	4	5	6	7	8	9	10	11	12	13	14	15
# of turns	14	2	5	7	4	5	3	1	4	1	2	0	2	0

Using this data, they could calculate that for every 50 plays, they would take in a total of $75 and give away $153.50 worth of prizes. They would therefore lose a lot of money should this represent what would occur at the actual fair. The students could then use their data to make modifications (for example, offer cheaper prizes, make it harder to win prizes, charge more to play the game, redesign the parachute so that it is harder to get high points) so that the game would make a profit. Naturally, a modification like redesigning the parachute or the target would require collecting new data to ensure that the new game would indeed make a reasonable profit. Students may not necessarily choose to do this if they run out of time, but they would need to raise these issues in their reflections.

Extensions

This task offers students an opportunity to apply their mathematical knowledge from many content domains. Students may greatly enjoy this task and wish to extend it beyond the requirements of the formal assessment (for example, try a number of different game designs, produce typewritten reports). Following the assessment, you may wish to conduct a class discussion in which students share their findings with each other, speculate about the reasons for differing results in their experimental data, and argue for a game design and a set of rules that they think will work best.

Task

Characterizing Performance

This section offers a characterization of student responses and provides indications of the ways in which the students were successful or unsuccessful in engaging with and completing the task. The descriptions are keyed to the *Core Elements of Performance.* Our global descriptions of student work range from "The student needs significant instruction" to "The student's work meets the essential demands of the task." Samples of student work that exemplify these descriptions of performance are included below, accompanied by commentary on central aspects of each student's response. These sample responses are *representative;* they may not mirror the global description of performance in all respects, being weaker in some and stronger in others.

The characterization of student responses for this task is based on these *Core Elements of Performance:*

1. Design a game within given parameters with clear and consistent rules.
2. Collect and organize experimental data.
3. Analyze data.
4. Interpret data to modify rules for a game.
5. Formulate further questions.
6. Communicate mathematical reasoning in support of choices.

Descriptions of Student Work

The group needs significant instruction.

Group fails to complete several pieces of the task (for example, the parachutes, target, rules, the data, reflection) or fails to consider *numerous* important parameters of the task (for example, game makes a profit, uses 5 rings for the target, parachutes are made from 3"-by-5" index cards, etc.).

No student examples at this level.

The group needs some instruction.

Group addresses parts of the task and demonstrates knowledge in a particular area, but fails to include major pieces of the task (for example, group does not collect experimental data).

Group A

This group addresses all parts of the task but does not gather experimental data, although in their reflections, they mention that this is necessary for constructing the best possible game. They do not include discussion about how the game could make money or how they could determine whether it would. They show a knowledge of circles in describing their target and their parachute design seems well suited to the game's objective—it lands unpredictably and cannot be aimed.

The group's work needs to be revised.

The group addresses all parts of the task, but lacks accuracy, completeness, or clarity in some important piece of the task (for example, experimental data may be incomplete or not clearly communicated).

No student examples at this level.

The group's work meets the essential demands of the task.

Group addresses all parts of the task, describes a logical and consistent game, and provides adequate support and justification.

Group B

This group shows use of reasoning and mathematical knowledge in addressing all parts of the task. They show consideration of possible variables in deciding upon the rules of the game (they specify the height of the chair, the distance of the chair from the target). They explain how the group members conducted experimental trials with two different parachutes and a number of target designs and how the group made decisions based on the results of those trials. The group also collected several sets of experimental data and used the data to determine the cost to play (although the group did not say how they used their results to determine this) and cost of prizes. The group determined a profit for thirty trials of three parachute drops each. In the reflections, the group discusses how certain tested variables may not mirror results at an actual carnival.

I. Parachutes:

First of all, to make a parachute you'll need a 3x5" Card. Round off the corners with sissors, starting from the middle of one of the shorter sides. cut an arc to about one inch from the other side, do the same on the opposite end. Pull the two thin sides together an put a paper clip on them to keep them together. After, color them and you are finished.

II. Target:

Using a sheet of white paper approximatly 27 inches wide by 33 inches long. Pick a point nearest the middle of the paper. With a compass, make a circle with a radius of about two inches. From the same point, make a concentric circle around the first one with a radius of about 4 inches. Make three more concentric circles, addindg two inches to the radius each time. Then color each ring with a different color to finish the target. The middle circle is labeled 100. the next one out is 75, then 50, 25 and the outer one is 10 points.

III. Rules:

To play the game, stand on a chair 17 inches from the ground. The parachute has to be dropped from a hieght of two yards off the ground.

The price to play is 30 cents for one parachute, 50 cents for two. On a turn, if the player gets less than 25 points they get small prize. If they get between 25 and 75 they get a medium prize and if the get 100 or more the win a large prize and a free turn. prizes may vary.

IV. Appendices:

On the parachutes sections, each of the people in our group made a parachute and we chose the best one.

On the Target section, our desicions were made by discussing desgins for our target, and when one desgin came up we discussed it.

On the Rules section, we wrote down some of the rules we thought were appropriate for the Section and discussed those.

V. Reflections:

Three issues that we ran into that would need further investigation in desging the best possible game would be, Testing the game over a length of time to see if it would be a good money maker, The target was too small and the parachute was too big, The prizes needed to be better quality (in other words less cheesey).

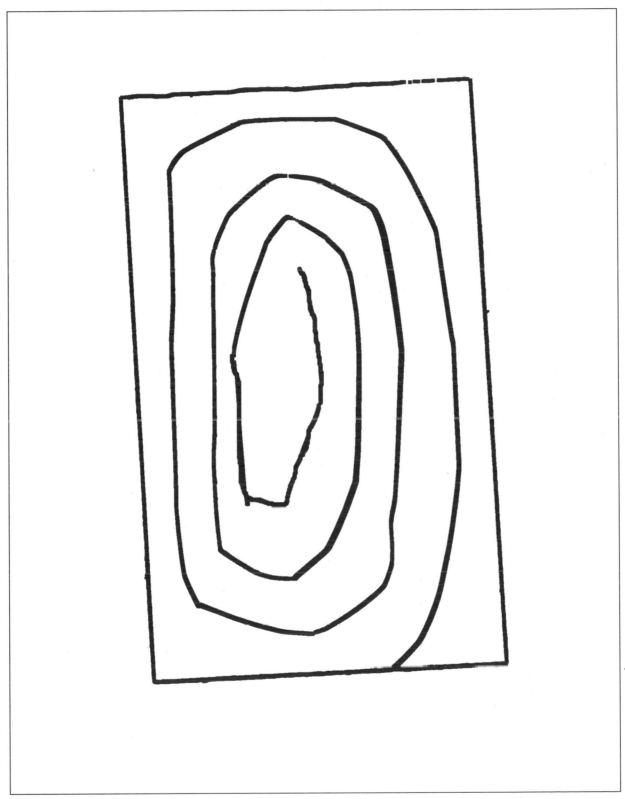

I. The Game

A. The Parachute

We tried three different types of parachutes. The first, we made a cut about one fifth of the way into the sheet all the way until about three inches away from the end. Do the same on the opposite side. Then there will be three fifths left, cut into thirds the same way.

Example:

Then connect the two outer flaps together with two paperclips. We thought that this was a good design because with the two paperclips, the parachute was weighted down, and therefore fell straight down.

For the second parachute, we did the same as above, but also connect the two inner flaps with two paperclips. This was a good design because it was a bit deceiving. It was deceiving because in our game to win, the paperclip hit the ring, with this parachute, it looked like you had two chances. It also fell straight down but also bounced, good for winning sometimes, but not all.

Group B

The third parachute we tried was cut in three inches from both sides, from there cut in toward the center two inches, Then fold these two strips together and hold together with two paperclips. This looks like an "H".

Example:

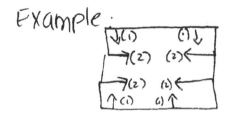

This was a good design because half of our tries (dropping parachute onto target) we scored.

B. The target that we used for our game is set up as follows:

ring 1 — worth 5 points
Diameter of 7cm

ring 2 — worth 4 points
Diameter of 13.5cm

ring 3 — worth 3 points
Diameter of 8.3cm

ring 4 — worth 2 points
Diameter of 24.2cm

ring 5 — worth 1 point
Diameter of 28.8cm

We tried two different targets. After thorough testing we decided that this target would end up making us more money. This target is also a good size for our game. Since we didn't have an actual basis for size of target to start with, we had to test each of our targets. This became the optimum target because while the target was not so big that everybody won, it was large enough to have approximately 1/2 of the people win something. Our other targets were either too big or too small and our decision was that they didn't even out the winnings enough.

C. The Rules:
We began by setting up the actual rules for the game. We stated these in a list form

and they showed what you could and could not do

Rule #1: players may pick where they hold the parachute.

Rule #2: Chair is placed 14 inches away from the target.

Rule #3: Chair used is 43cm high.

Rule #4: Person dropping must have both feet all the way on the chair.

Rule #5: Arm must be held at shoulder height of Contestant

Rule #6: Contestant must stand up straight

After determining all of the rules, we had to decide how much people would win and how much the prizes we gave would cost us.

To find out what we wanted to spend on prices, once again we tested our situation. After attempting 50 turns just as an average contestant would do. Upon finding our results, we determined that someone should have to pay one dollar to drop 3 times. If your total score for the three times was 7, you won 8 tickets

We were able to   8-9, you won 9 tickets
determine this   10-15, you won 10 tickets
after deciding how much each prize we gave away would be worth in actual money that it would cost us and in tickets. The contestants would win.

Group B

prize	cost of prizes for us	amount of tickets prize costs for contestants
dum dum	one cent	one ticket
blow pops	15 cents	2 tickets
funsize candy bar	25 cents	5 tickets
full size candy bar	40 cents	8 tickets
lolly pops	50 cents	10 tickets
King size candy bar	50 cents	10 tickets
poster	one dollar	25 tickets
mini squirt guns	one dollar	25 tickets
small dolls	75 dollar	20 tickets
whoopie cushions	one dollar	25 tickets

This cost for prizes and tickets per prize gave people the thought that they were winning and also gave us the premium amount of profit.

Group B

II The Data: The results

A

Data for how to Score how many trys the player gets and the cost to play.

First Taved stood on a chair 43cm tall The chair was placed 42 cm away from the target-

Taved is 6ft. tall.

He used Parachute #2 when he was standing on the chair his feet did not go over the edge and he held his arm out at shoulder length. His arm wasn't bent or exactly straight, it was just relaxed. The results are below. A try equals one drop and the points represent what ring the paperclip rested in. Since there are 2 places on the Parachute with paper clips on them we counted the highest point value.

TRy	Points
1	2 pts
2	2 pts
3	1 pt
4	2 pts
5	out (0pts)
6	out
7	out
8	3 pts
9	out
10	out

min. – Opts

max. – 3 pts

Aug – 1 Pt

Total – 10 pts

Then Katie did exactly the same thing, but she is 5 ft 5 in. Her resuls are below:

Try	Points
1	4 pts
2	2 pts
3	5 pts
4	Out

Try	Points
5	Out
6	Out
7	Out
8	Out

Try	Points
9	1 pt.
10	2 pts.

Over →

from Katies table on the other side)

$$\underline{min} - out$$
$$\underline{max} - 5 \, pts.$$
$$\underline{Avg.} - 14 \, pts$$
$$\underline{Total} - 14 \, pts$$

using the information from above we decided that each player would pay $1.00 for 3 drops and that to win you had to have atleast 7 pts. The table below is a table for the total points each person got in 1 trial. A trial is 3 drops.

Trial (3 drops)	Beth	Katie	Taved
1	1	6	7 ✶
2	0	7 ✶	1
3	8 ✶	0	8 ✶
4	1	4	7 ✶
5	2	4	4
6	6	1	0
7	10	0	0
8	3	3	7 ✶
9	6	0	0
10	8 ✶	2	5

✶ = A win

The table below is of the prizes we decided to use, the estimated cost of each (when bought in bulk), and how many tickets you need to win that prize.

points Earned	tickets earned
7 pts	8
8-9 pts	9
10-15 pts	10

more →

Group B

Prize	Cost for us	how many tickets
dum dum	1¢	1
blow pop	15¢	2
fun size candy bar	25¢	5
lolly pops	50¢	10
King size candy bar	50¢	10
poster	$1	25
mini squirt gun	$1	25
little dolls	75¢	20
whoople cushion	$1	25
candy bar	40¢	8

Below is a table of Income + profit —

Tared	Katie	Beth
$10 to play— $1.41 (prize cost) = $8.59	$10 to play – 40¢ (prize cost) = $9.60	$10.00 to play = $1.16 (prize cost) = $8.84

from all of the combined data we determined that out of $30 dollars of income we would make a profit of about $27.03

B) Interpretation

The object of this project was to make money and the secound Parachute would do this. We picked this one because it landed fifty percent of the time in the target. and fifty percent of the time it landed outside of the target. Since there are two ends with papeclips people will think that they have a double chance of winning. Sometimes it bounced and it would go out or in and we counted where the resting spot was. If both paper clips landed in the player could pick which score they wanted.

Reflections:

With a game like this, several problems could occur. This game is based on a given climate. If the carnival where this game was being played happened to be outside, it would become nearly impossible to win if there was any sort of breeze. This breeze could easily throw your results off. Another major thing that is not a definite is the cost of the prizes. Our group decided on what prizes we wanted to give away but we were unable to do any research on actual cost of these prizes to get a more accurate picture of the amount of income and profit. One would need to find factual data. For example, we estimated that we could buy these for 40 cents but that was our estimate.

The last thing that is uncertain is that we have no gurantee that people are going to play the game and who is going to play the game. In the end, we may find that we need to charge more to play the game. We may find that not enough people play the game to make the desired amount of profit. This data can be found only by results of the game at carnivals. If enough people come, we make enough of a percent of profit to get enough money but if not enough come. the possibility of not making enough money is there.

Through testing, all of these problems can be solved or overcome. This does not change the fact that there will be problems but they are all problems that can be solved through the proper amounts of research.

Glossary

This glossary defines a number of the terms that are used to describe the *Dimensions of Balance* table that appears in the package *Introduction*.

Applied power: a task goal—to provide students an opportunity to demonstrate their power over a real-world practical situation, with that as the main criterion for success. This includes choosing mathematical tools appropriately for the problem situation, using them effectively, and interpreting and evaluating the results in relation to the practical needs of the situation. [cf. *illustrative application*]

Checking and evaluating: a mathematical process that involves evaluating the quality of a problem solution in relation to the problem situation (for example, checking calculations; comparing model predictions with data; considering whether a solution is reasonable and appropriate; asking further questions).

Definition of concepts: a task type—such tasks require the clarification of a concept and the generation of a mathematical definition to fit a set of conditions.

Design: a task type that calls for the design, and perhaps construction, of an object (for example, a model building, a scale drawing, a game) together with instructions on how to use the object. The task may include evaluating the results in light of various constraints and desirable features. [cf. *plan*]

Evaluation and recommendation: a task type that calls for collecting and analyzing information bearing on a decision. Students review evidence and make a recommendation based on the evidence. The product is a "consultant" report for a "client."

Exercise: a task type that requires only the application of a learned procedure or a "tool kit" of techniques (for example, adding decimals; solving an equation); the product is simply an answer that is judged for accuracy.

Illustrative application of mathematics: a task goal—to provide the student an opportunity to demonstrate effective use of mathematics in a context outside mathematics. The focus is on the specific piece of mathematics, while the reality and utility of the context as a model of a practical situation are secondary. [cf. *applied power*]

Inferring and drawing conclusions: a mathematical process that involves applying derived results to the original problem situation and interpreting the results in that light.

Modeling and formulating: a mathematical process that involves taking the situation as presented in the task and formulating mathematical statements of the problem to be solved. Working the task involves selecting appropriate representations and relationships to model the problem situation.

Nonroutine problem: a task type that presents an unfamiliar problem situation, one that students are not expected to have analyzed before or have not met regularly in the curriculum. Such problems demand some flexibility of thinking, and adaptation or extension of previous knowledge. They may be situated in a context that students have not encountered in the curriculum; they may involve them in the introduction of concepts and techniques that will be explicitly taught at a later stage; they may involve the discovery of connections among mathematical ideas.

Open-ended: a task structure that requires some questions to be posed by the student. Therefore open-ended tasks often have multiple solutions and may allow for a variety of problem-solving strategies. They provide students with a wide range of possibilities for choosing and making decisions. [cf. *open-middle*]

Open investigation: an open-ended task type that invites exploration of a problem situation with the aim of discovering and establishing facts and relationships. The criteria for evaluating student performance are based on exploring thoroughly, generalizing, justifying, and explaining with clarity and economy.

Open-middle: a task structure in which the question and its answer are well-defined (there is a clear recognizable "answer") but with a variety of strategies or methods for approaching the problem. [cf. *open-ended*]

Plan: a task type that calls for the design of a sequence of activities, or a schedule of events, where time is an essential variable and where the need to organize the efforts of others is implied. [cf. *design*]

Pure mathematics: a task type—one that provides the student an opportunity to demonstrate power over a situation within a mathematics "microworld." This may be an open investigation, a nonroutine problem, or a technical exercise.

Reporting: a mathematical process that involves communicating to a specified "audience" what has been learned about the problem. Components of a successful response include explaining why the results follow from the problem formulation, explaining manipulations of the formalism, and drawing conclusions from the information presented, with some evaluation.

Re-presentation of information: a task type that requires interpretation of information presented in one form and its translation to some different form (for example, write a set of verbal directions that would allow a listener to reproduce a given geometric design; represent the information in a piece of text with a graphic or a symbolic expression).

Review and critique: a task type that involves reflection on curriculum materials (for example, one might review a piece of student work, identify errors, and make suggestions for revision; pose further questions; produce notes on a recently learned topic).

Scaffolding: the degree of detailed step-by-step guidance that a task prompt provides a student.

Task length: the time that should be allowed for students to work on the task. Also important is the length of time students are asked by the task to think independently—the reasoning length. (For a single well-defined question, reasoning length will equal the task length; for a task consisting of many parts, the reasoning length can be much shorter—essentially the time for the longest part.)

Transforming and manipulating: a mathematical process that involves manipulating the mathematical forms in which the problem is expressed, usually with the aim of transforming them into other equivalent forms that represent "solutions" to the problem (for example, dividing one fraction by another, making a geometric construction, solving equations, plotting graphs, finding the derivative of a function).